D0203720

COLLECTIVE BARGAINING IN STATE AND LOCAL GOVERNMENT

COLLECTIVE BARGAINING IN STATE AND LOCAL GOVERNMENT

John Patrick Piskulich

PRAEGER

New York
Westport, Connecticut
London

Library of Congress Cataloging-in-Publication Data

Piskulich, John Patrick.
    Collective bargaining in state and local government / John Patrick Piskulich.
        p.   cm.
    Includes bibliographical references and index.
    ISBN 0-275-94043-8 (alk. paper)
    1. Collective bargaining–State government employees–United States.   2. Collective
bargaining–Government employees–United States.   3. Employee-management relations in
government–United States.   I. Title.
    HD8005.6.U5P57   1992
    331.89′04135′0000973–dc20   91-28142

British Library Cataloguing in Publication Data is available.

Library of Congress Catalog Card Number: 91-28142
ISBN: 0-275-94043-8

First published in 1992

Praeger Publishers, One Madison Avenue, New York, NY 10010
An imprint of Greenwood Publishing Group, Inc.

Printed in the United States of America

∞™

The paper used in this book complies with the
Permanent Paper Standard issued by the National
Information Standards Organization (Z39.48-1984).

10 9 8 7 6 5 4 3 2 1

To Mary Anne

From the other side of the table

Contents

Tables and Figures

TABLES

FIGURES

COLLECTIVE BARGAINING
IN STATE AND
LOCAL GOVERNMENT

1 Introduction

Unions in the United States are not dead. They may not be strong, or even particularly healthy. However, the sometimes-hoped-for and much-predicted demise of the American labor movement has not yet come to pass.

Why the negative predictions? Maybe we misinterpret the statistics, or perhaps we allow fear and easy pessimism to cloud our view of the future. To the satisfaction of some and to the dismay of others, a common characterization is that labor is merely "a shell of its former self." To substantiate this claim, adherents to this view cite, among other things, more frequent concession bargaining and the steady decline in private sector union membership of recent decades. The latter trend undoubtedly receives the most attention, but it builds no more than a weak case for labor's impending demise because it neglects an important part of the tale.

Though labor may now claim only approximately seventeen percent of the private sector workforce, we seem to forget three things. First, the unionized segment was never more than thirty-five percent of the total at its peak. Second, the present figure remains a sizeable, if declining, proportion. Third, there is not a direct arithmetic correspondence between group size and social, economic, or political clout.

Most visible for its absence in the generalization is the public sector component of the labor movement. About half of those employed at all levels of government are represented by a labor organization, and more than a third are union members.

Perhaps the negative predictions about the labor movement are rooted in the fear of uncertainty, which leads to pessimism about the future. Maybe it is fear of a new economic reality, an impending order to our world that we may not like very much or that we may not be able to live with once it arrives.

Headlines and public opinion polls indicate that, among other concerns, Americans are increasingly worried about two things: "The Deficit" and "The Japanese." The former threatens our domestic living standards and the latter portends an end to Pax Americana. Fear of the deficit, it can be argued, may be less the perception of a real threat than it is the use of a convenient label, grasped of necessity, to articulate our underlying anxieties about living in an era of limits—the resource scarcity of Thurow's (1980) zero-sum society. The allocation of loss is not easy or pleasant. Fear of the Japanese also puts a face on the turbulence of international markets, wrought (according to many) by that side of the globe.

Others look for culprits closer to home. If concern about the deficit and the Japanese are merely tangible manifestations of a more fundamental unease about the future, union-bashing seems to be a phenomenon cut from the same cloth. "It's the unions . . ." remains something of a boilerplate attribution of blame for many of our economic troubles. The conventional wisdom often posits an inverse relationship between economic growth (both at home and abroad) and union power. Such beliefs, though deterministic, do betray the fact that unions remain strong enough to make many of us uneasy.

In the private sector, ask Frank Lorenzo. Lorenzo gained the admiration of some for "standing up to the unions" at Continental, while earning the contempt of others for "standing behind Chapter 11." The battle escalated at Eastern, another subsidiary of Lorenzo's Texas Air. Disharmony is not limited to one company: labor-management disputes continue to plague Carl Icahn at TWA. Nor is it specific to the airline industry: only the improved health of automakers (afforded, in part, by congressional protection from imports) relieved much of the pressure on and from the UAW during the middle 1980s.

In the public sector, ask any mayor or city manager. The spectre of an entire community without fire or police protection, trash heaped at every curb, or children out of school for extended periods haunts even the most firmly entrenched of their number—particularly in an election year. Former Chicago Mayor Mike Bilandic can testify that disruption of a somewhat less compelling service like snow removal can actually have quite dramatic electoral significance.

In both sectors, public and private, unions make others of us uneasy because they impede unilateral action by the employer. Equalizing the disparity in bargaining power between the individual, acting alone, and employer monopsony in the labor market was, of course, one rationale for the legislation that brought collective bargaining to the private sector: Norris-LaGuardia (1932), Wagner (1935), Taft-Hartley (1947), and Landrum-Griffin (1959). If we chafe at being hamstrung, it is because we forget the tradeoff inherent in these statutes. Management prerogative had to be constrained through collective action by labor if we were to reap the benefits embodied in our goals of (1) labor peace, through institutionalized mechanisms of communication, (2) workplace democracy and self-governance, and (3) pluralism, or effective political representation by unions as interest groups (Wellington and Winter, 1969; 1970; 1971).

It is not entirely surprising that we might not remember the bargain we struck. The labor "movement" may now be something of an anachronism since the deaths of Debs, Hoffa, and Meany or as the unrest of the IWW, the Haymarket riot, and the Boston police strike recedes into memory. The streets are quiet now.

Other observers appear to remember the past, but argue the wisdom of these policy decisions. The experience of more than a half-century of collective bargaining, critics contend, indicates that the economic and social costs of our actions by now outweigh the benefits. The essence of their argument is that the pendulum swings too far toward the labor end of its arc, despite efforts to negotiate more flexible work rules and to rein in "fat" and "corrupt" labor leadership. The result is economic stagnation at home and an inability to compete in world markets. They believe the social impact to be equally unacceptable. The legal problems of the last five Teamsters presidents, they suggest, are testimony to labor's embedded corruption. Jimmy Hoffa disappeared, but his legacy remains with us.

Organized labor is not without its supporters. What this camp fears most is unrestrained managerial discretion over compensation and working conditions. If they share a banner, it reads "what management gives, management may take away," a proverb often employed in skirmishes with their opponents. The textile industry is a traditional site for many such intellectual battles. Supporters maintain that for every "success story" like Hanes (labor peace without unions) there exists a J.P. Stevens (the thinly veiled company in "Norma Rae"), and the potential for many more (enter the proverb). Management is benevolent only when it can afford to be.

In addition, the cost-benefit calculus of the prolabor camp leads to a decidedly different conclusion about the social utility of collective bargaining. Some are willing to bear Teamster-like abuses because they go so far as to attribute much of America's post-Depression political stability directly to the strength of organized labor. Economist Barry Bluestone contends that realizing the "American dream" of home ownership in the suburbs was only possible for a large segment of our society through union jobs and union incomes. Organized labor lubricates the system, an important channel of upward social mobility responsible for creating a middle class to span the gap between the economic elite and the working class and promising a piece of the dream to blue collar Americans sure to be excluded otherwise (Cook, 1983; Bluestone and Harrison, 1982).

At the heart of this debate lie fundamental disputes over the economic and social impacts of the private sector labor relations model. These disputes carry over and become more complex when the subject is the public sector. They carry over because we basically expropriated the private sector system for public sector use (lacking a ready alternative), and they become more complex because of the interaction between politics and economics.

ECONOMIC THEORY: THE PRIVATE SECTOR

Economic theory identifies some short-run social costs associated with the advent of collective bargaining. Increased labor costs without a concomitant increase in output results in decreased productivity and therefore suboptimal performance of the economy. The model also forsees potential price instability, to the extent that these increases limit competition to a smaller number of firms (those able to afford higher labor costs) with larger market shares and therefore greater discretionary impact on the market itself.

Theory indicates, on the other hand, that long-run competition should limit the economic costs of bargaining. The work of Alfred Marshall informs us that the demand for labor is indirect, derived from the demand for those products to which it is applied (*Principles of Economics*, 1936). Labor's demand schedule is also its marginal revenue product (MRP) schedule (depicted in figure 1.1). Assuming enough competition that a single employer cannot affect the market wage rate, market constraint upon wages is imposed in the form of a wage-employment tradeoff. Up to point E in figure 1.1, the added revenue brought in by an additional worker is greater than her wage, so she is adding to profit. Beyond E,

Figure 1.1
The Wage-Employment Tradeoff

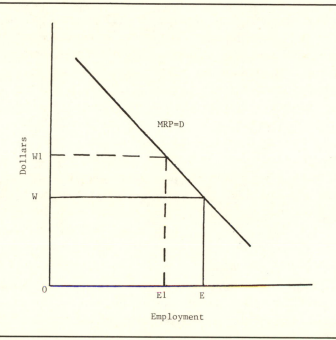

Source: Reynolds, Lloyd G., Stanley H. Masters, and Colletta H. Moser, Labor Economics and Labor Relations, 1st edition, © 1991, p. 119. Reprinted by permission of Prentice Hall, Englewood Cliffs, New Jersey.

however, an additional worker contributes less than her wage, so profit is reduced. If the wage rate is increased from W to W1, E1 becomes the appropriate level of employment. The MRP schedule, then, charts the tradeoffs between wage and employment levels faced by labor.

This curve is not fixed, however. The demand for labor varies with (1) the elasticity of demand for the product, (2) the degree to which labor is an essential factor in the production process, (3) the cost of labor relative to the total cost of production, and (4) the supply of alternative factors of production, such as capital or alternative (i.e., non-union) forms of labor. As competition increases, the profit-maximizing firm has greater incentive to substitute capital for labor or to employ less costly labor (often in the non-union South or overseas). In this way, competition exerts downward pressure on wages, or alternatively, market-imposed unemployment results as labor costs increase (Reynolds et al., 1991).

ECONOMIC THEORY: THE PUBLIC SECTOR

In the case of the public sector we make different predictions, primarily because of an expected change in the slope of the demand curve. To continue the line of argument outlined by Wellington and Winter that appears above, the initial three of the four claims for (or goals of) bargaining in the private sector (i.e., industrial peace, industrial democracy, effective political representation, and unequal bargaining power) apply equally well to the public sector. Labor peace is obviously desirable in our public organizations, and we also recognize the utility of collective action for providing our employees with a sense of self-governance and/ or control over their destiny. (In fact, the latter concern may be all the more compelling as larger and more complex bureaucratic organizations develop.) Yet public diverges from private when the question of bargaining power is considered.

Collective bargaining in the public sector can be considered less an economic relationship than a manifestly *political* interaction. The wage-employment tradeoff changes character to the extent that most governmental activity is monopolistic in nature. That is, a dearth of alternative service providers means that the demand for services like police and fire protection is less elastic (or more inelastic): it is less sensitive to changes in price. Local governments can rarely afford to buy fewer police, firefighters, or teachers, even if their "price" rises.

While there will be some situations in which a fear of unemployment restrains the willingness of public employees to exert upward pressure on wages, political considerations are likely to play a mitigating role. For example, a fixed budget necessitates layoffs as labor costs increase. However, a decline in personnel threatens the scope and quality of service delivery, making unions and service beneficiaries natural allies. The impact of such layoffs on the local unemployment rate may also deter elected officials from assuming a tough fiscal stance.

ALTERNATIVES

Do governors and mayors have other options? Maybe. They might try to substitute capital for labor. Visions of "Robocop" are darkly amusing, but the general idea may not be as farfetched as it appears. A few bold states are supplementing state troopers with less obtrusive speed-sensitive cameras on their highways. Currently in the experimental phase, it remains to be seen whether such a strategy, once formally adopted, will lead to personnel reductions or instead to the reassignment of displaced troopers to the trails of more pernicious criminals.[1]

The privatization of public services (an attempt to inject market discipline) may be another attractive strategy for gaining a grip on high labor costs. Debate now centers on the details of its implementation. Here, too, concerns about feasibility and desirability loom large. Questions of accountability in particular (e.g., elected officials held responsible for the quality of services over which they possess diminished control; the size of the public monitoring apparatus required) complicate estimates of cost savings.

What of the long run? The Tiebout hypothesis (1956) argues that long-term population mobility also extenuates upward pressure on public sector labor costs. Residents of a jurisdiction confronted with declines in service or, alternatively, higher tax bills to continue service at present levels will exercise their exit option: they vote with their feet. State and local policymakers face something of a double-edged sword here, encapsulating what may be characterized as a "crisis of fiscal federalism" (Reagan and Sanzone, 1981). Governors in particular encounter, on one hand, the prospect of increased reliance upon own-source revenues, as the deficit and a change in philosophy at the national level result in curtailed federal aid to subnational jurisdictions. On the other, they face a public which expects to receive service at present or improved levels of quantity and quality. Arizona Governor Bruce Babbit remarked at the time that the early effort of the Reagan administration to consolidate a series of categorical grants into a smaller number of block grants was "a tactical weapon to cut the federal budget while deputizing governors to hand out the bad news" (Stanfield, 1981, p. 1800).

What if elected representatives cannot find a way to make the bad news palatable for their constituents? They are forced to do more with less. If services cannot be cut or taxes increased, then the apparent solution is to do the job more efficiently and effectively. Retrenchment of this sort provides the major impetus for productivity improvement efforts. In the labor relations context, such a strategy is manifested in calls for "productivity bargaining," in which employee compensation is contractually tied to changes in negotiated productivity indicators.

Yet there is another more fundamental, potentially effective, and intuitively appealing alternative available to policymakers faced with an organized cadre of public employees seeking regular increases in remuneration. Crudely stated, the policy prescription is to "cut them off at the knees." Statutory provisions designed to circumscribe (if not to negate) the bargaining power of those sitting across the negotiating table (or for that matter, to keep them from the table entirely) are fairly common. A ban on strikes attempts to shoot this trump from the hand of labor. Right-to-Work laws try to keep labor from even pulling up a chair.

The need to curtail excessive union influence over a shrinking pie may be quite salable to a public uneasy about its economic future. Indeed, policy is often a blunt instrument forged in the fires of uncertainty. It is precisely because this last option seems so blunt that its elaboration is in order.

PLURALISM AND DEMOCRACY

To rely upon Wellington and Winter another time, policymakers justify strike bans for "essential" services in order to ensure the survival of the "normal" political process. The pluralist perspective of American democracy (Bentley, 1908; Truman, 1951; Dahl, 1961) maintains that there is a high probability that any active and legitimate group can achieve voice in the decision-making process. Yet given the inelasticity of demand for public services, so the argument goes, the ability to strike confers disproportionate power upon labor; organized public employees possess this weapon over and above others in their arsenal available for exerting more typical political pressure to get what they want from the public employer. This skews the normal pluralist operation of the system to the extent that other groups seeking a portion of the fiscal pie face a significant competitive disadvantage. As a police, firefighter, teacher, or sanitation strike wears on, the negative reaction of voters to the inconvenience or danger associated with disrupted service generates a great deal of political pressure for a settlement, regardless of its cost. Protecting the budget from becoming a union hostage is thereby used to justify the strike ban.

LIMITS OF THE MODEL

There are limits to this progression of logic. Most apparent may be the question of public reaction. Citizens of any jurisdiction expect effective uniformed services, they take pride in good schools, and they understand the need to provide their public servants with reasonable compensation for the functions they perform in the community. While these values may lead them to tolerate the inconvenience associated with the occasional short-term strike, their patience will wear thin as disruptions become more frequent or of longer duration. Fear of unpatrolled streets, unattended fires, uneducated children, and unsanitary trash piled at the curb can become quite compelling. Those affected may pay the bill to resolve the immediate crisis, but they may not forget its initiator. Widespread public irritation associated with lengthy and recurring strikes by teachers in Chicago and in Detroit are two recent examples. The point to be made is that even in the absence of a ban, the decision to strike cannot be taken lightly by labor leadership. It almost always involves a tradeoff between economic gain in the short term and a loss of goodwill in the future. Taxpayers will resent feeling manipulated; before they deplete this capital of support, labor must factor the future impact of sustained anti-union sentiment into their strike calculus.[2]

It may also be the case that public employee unions must worry about more than just taxpayer opposition. Extending Truman's conception of latent groups to this context, Chimezie A.B. Osigweh (1985) makes the theoretical argument that the pluralistic political process in "the world's number one democracy" remains an effective check on union power (p. 82). Reactive counter groups of all sorts emerge to impose "appropriate" checks and balances upon unions engaging in "heartless bargaining" or achieving "outlandish gains." Fearing such backlash, the latter are likely to exercise restraint and temper their demands not only to prevent vociferous taxpayer opposition, but also to moderate efforts directed against them by business and other groups.

Beyond the political realm, Osigweh reexamines the economic and financial contexts of public sector collective bargaining. As in the former case, he identifies a number of reasons to question the Wellington and Winter model and therefore few reasons to substantiate common and persistent unease about the potential power of unions in the public sphere.

Osigweh finds four reasons to question the conventional economic wisdom. First, previous estimates of demand elasticity (e.g., Ashenfelter and Ehrenberg, 1975) may be overstated. Observed declines in the level of government employment across various subnational jurisdictions (Weitzman, 1979; Schlosstein, 1975) and the impact of actual or threatened efforts at subcontracting public services (e.g., Burton and Krider, 1972) appear to indicate greater sensitivity to the price of labor than that witnessed in the previous research.

Second, not all services are "essential." Variation in the use of injunctions (Aboud and Aboud, 1974) and in the probability that the public employer will seek replacement personnel (Burton and Krider, 1972) in order to forestall strikes is used as evidence for this claim.

Third, the labor-intensive nature of most public services (as above) means that payroll costs account for a sizeable proportion of subnational budgets. Since labor costs comprise as much as 70 percent of local expenditures, any increase is quite visible and will be felt by elected officials and by the general public. Both therefore have strong incentive to resist this upward pressure, even in the short run.

This high labor-to-total cost ratio provides Osigweh with a fourth reason to question the traditional public sector economic model. Experience in private sector manufacturing indicates that compensation levels are closely tied to changes in productivity (Kochan, 1980; Freedman, 1979). We know from the previous discussion that the public employer has a difficult time substituting alternative factors of production (i.e., capital) for police officers, firefighters, and teachers. This leads to the conclusion that remuneration is likely to be constrained (relative to the private sector) regardless of union activity, to the extent that public productivity is limited by this inability to adopt technological innovations.

Finally, Osigweh's analysis of the financial context is congruent with the earlier observation that the public employer is indeed trapped in a fiscal bind. Not only do subnational public administrators face the reality of diminished intergovernmental assistance, but they are assaulted from all sides, "caught between employee compensation demands, public willingness to vote for increased operating levies, shrinking tax bases, opposition interests, and the legislatures' reluctance to allow governments the freedom to impose any kind of tax(es) at will" (p. 80). The result: unions face a harried employer with strong incentive to take a rigorous bargaining stance. It is a much tougher battle at the negotiating table.

COMPETING PERSPECTIVES

Policymakers and policy analysts therefore find themselves in something of a theoretical muddle, confronted with conflicting hypotheses and mixed empirical evidence about the mechanics of collective bargaining in the public sector. Unclear patterns in the data inhibit their ability to formulate policy and policy recommendations, respectively, with satisfactory confidence. Both are ambivalent because they recognize the implications of the potential tradeoff, a tension between the costs and benefits associated with institutionalized checks on union strength of greater or lesser magnitude.

If stiff constitutional or statutory provisions are devised to check union power, the risk is that the leverage public employees can exert in the negotiations process will be annulled, thereby removing the incentive for employees to act in a "collective" fashion and deleting the "bargaining" from collective bargaining. Unilateral management discretion displaces mutual agreement. Thus, the benefits to be accrued from collective bar-

gaining are forfeited, the potential to improve the quality of public organizations through bilateral determination of wages and working
conditions lost. Substantial opportunity costs are thereby incurred if such
a policy strategy is adopted.

At the other pole resides unilateralism of the opposite sort. Unchecked,
strong public employee unions may use their weapons to extort an increasingly larger share of the public purse. The scenario feared most is
the one in which the *de facto* power of labor effectively overwhelms *de
jure* legislative authority over the appropriations process. This is the
policy option that leads to the debate over sovereignty alluded to previously, a delegation question. To the extent that one competitor for a
public good exerts disproportionate power over its allocation, the political
process and the public good are subverted.

SOVEREIGNTY

Perhaps most interesting is the debate about whether or not "the sovereignty issue" remains an issue at all. In fact, this dispute lies at the
heart of the policy dilemma public jurisdictions now encounter. Despite
reports to the contrary, this question is still very much alive. There are
at least three schools of thought at work here. Arguing what appears to
be the dominant position, Freeman (1986) contends (in the Wellington
and Winter tradition) that the issue "has, for the most part, been resolved"
through legislation prohibiting strikes for "essential service" employees
(pp. 50–51).

The second line of thinking maintains that policymakers are not consistent in their application of this philosophy from a systemic perspective,
and also questions the necessity of the strike ban in the public bargaining
context. Osigweh is not persuaded by the sovereignty argument on four
counts. The fact that suits (i.e., torts) may be initiated in instances of
government negligence indicates that the state does not possess blanket
sovereign immunity. Second, defense and other contractors may negotiate
terms of construction, delivery, and price for the goods and services they
provide public agencies without any apparent abdication of responsibility.
Third, Osigweh believes it "quite possible to isolate government's administrative responsibilities from those that are policymaking or legislative" (p. 81); the point is moot if we employ this distinction.[3] His final
criticism is that the people are the true sovereign, and they may certainly
decide to provide their employees with more power in the bargaining
relationship.

The third school emerges from an entirely different perspective. The belief here is that sovereignty is threatened even in the presence of policy mechanisms designed to limit union power. Unionized public employees retain excessive power; strikes continue to occur in the face of various penalties, and the union negotiator sits across the table from a bargaining agent with fragmented authority and limited incentive to resist labor demands on behalf of a rationally disinterested public (Baird, 1986; Conant, 1989).

In essence, the Freeman logic is satisfied with the strike ban while the other two schools are not, for very different reasons. The Osigweh camp believes that popular unease is unfounded because pluralism is naturally self-correcting: democracy will survive because it has to, not because strikes are prohibited. The third perspective asserts that even greater protection from union power is required, more than policy now provides. Reconciling these competing perspectives obviously hinges upon empirical estimates of both union power and the effectiveness of the present policy course (e.g., strike prohibitions).

ADDITIONAL VALUE CONFLICTS

We might take a moment to illuminate some of the additional value conflicts obscured thus far. If effectiveness is to be used as a criterion for assessing the current policy wisdom, another look at goals is in order. The "claims for bargaining" proposed by Wellington and Winter appear innocuous enough; we might all applaud the desire to achieve industrial peace, industrial democracy, effective political representation, and countervailing economic power. However, these are only *intermediate* goals, and they may in fact be something of a smokescreen behind which alternative political forces reside. In order to answer the question "To what end?" a broader, if typically neglected dimension of political economy must be addressed.

The assumptions behind these goals constitute the first issue here. Do policymakers pursue more efficient organizations through collective bargaining, or is it social equity they seek? Many economists, of course, see no normative conflict between equity and efficiency. In their universe, the former is an end and the latter is a means (i.e., the efficient allocation of resources, from a macroeconomic perspective, results in systemic social justice). Others have a different view. They worry first that this macro perspective contains no minimum standard of living (i.e., that some segment of the population is efficiently allocated *out* of full participation in society). This latter group is also concerned about intention: are labor peace and worker self-determination pursued in order to achieve organizational goals, political ends, or is the explicit aim to provide workers with the basic economic rights requisite to any "just" society? It would be easier to believe that organizational, political, and individual needs dovetail, but some analysts remain skeptical.

The substance of this skepticism encompasses two dimensions. The first is political. It is not difficult to argue that collective bargaining came to the private sector (i.e., Wagner) as much because of FDR's desire to include labor in the New Deal coalition as because of a reaction to pre-Depression labor strife (e.g., the Haymarket riot and the Boston police strike) or explicit philosophical sympathy with the working class.[4] This strategy was not costless for FDR; he was bitterly resented in labor-intensive sectors of the economy such as autos and steel (Ginsberg and Shefter, 1988, p. 212). However, a healthy postwar domestic economy and American domination of convalescing international markets went a long way toward healing this wound. America did, of course, sow the seeds of her present unease about union power. By helping to rebuild the European and Japanese economies, she also helped to create the international competition which now exerts such pressure on organized labor.

The second reason for skepticism reflects a traditional critique of organizational humanism (Denhardt, 1984, p. 97). The substance of this concern is that employees are provided with the bargaining status to assume a greater participatory role in the organization less because they possess any significant right to control their collective destiny than because it serves organizational purposes. The promise of countervailing economic power is merely a cooptative mechanism, a subtle tool of managerial control in the quest for greater operational efficiency. Greater efficiency may be achieved, but in no case will co-equal status be conferred; it is management alone which reaps the full rewards of bilateralism.

The essence of the argument, then, is that there is an equity obligation which transcends economic efficiency, a value scheme which cannot be ignored. A system of labor-management relations is not established merely because it can be afforded; tough economic times require joint solutions, not a rethinking of the ground rules. This line of thinking therefore deems it important not only that collective bargaining be institutionalized, but that it be done for the right reasons.

There is at least one other value conflict which further complicates the tension faced by policymakers. The concern here may best be characterized as one of "relative" equity, a question of employee rights across public and private sectors. To the extent that various bargaining practices are prohibited based upon employer, public servants are denied rights possessed by their private sector counterparts (e.g., the ability to engage in legal strikes). The dispute revolves around whether the classic distinctions in inelasticity, essentiality, or sovereignty are valid justifications for differential treatment. In the case of the strike ban, the objection typically takes one of three forms: (1) that the right to withhold labor is a fundamental and inherent right of any employee, (2) that policy is inconsistent, permitting the strike for private sector employees performing functions also found in the public sector, such as mass transit, health care, and education, or (3) that policy is inconsistent within the public sector itself to the extent that the essentiality distinction is employed (Cayer, 1986; Gordon, 1986; Shafritz et al., 1986). The general criticism is thus one of red lights placed at arbitrary intersections.

Achieving a balance between management prerogative and employee rights is obviously difficult, and it is fair to say that a judicially defined sphere of public employee rights, duties, and obligations continues to evolve. The issue remains salient because the "doctrine of privilege" utilized by the courts for so long in public personnel matters has not yet receded from memory. Although subsequently replaced by judicial constructions more favorable to members of the public workforce, Hatch restrictions upon federal employees are a continuing reminder of Justice Holmes's logic.

SUMMARY AND RESEARCH AGENDA

To recapitulate, Wellington and Winter describe four traditional claims for collective bargaining: (1) labor peace, (2) self-determination, (3) pluralism, and (4) unequal bargaining power. While valid in the private sector, this model diverges in the public case at (4) because of a (theorized) change in elasticity. Assuming that a difference in elasticity does indeed exist across the two sectors, the ability of the employer to resist bargaining demands differs as well. In the case of the private sector, management can (1) buy less labor as the price increases, (2) substitute capital, (3) employ cheaper labor, and/or (4) demand increased productivity. In the public sector the potential responses are different to the extent that this employer may (1) cut services, (2) substitute capital, (3) create a "market" through privatization, (4) await the long-term (Tiebout) adjustment, (5) demand increased productivity, and/or (6) manage/regulate the bargaining process in some fashion.

It is this last alternative (6) which the following research addresses. It should be clear from this chapter that a great deal of uncertainty plagues attempts by decision makers to formulate a workable system of labor-management relations in the public sector. We unquestionably paint with broad brush. If it is clear that policymakers face some difficult choices, it should be equally apparent that the solution to the muddle is not likely to lie at either of the extremes: debilitated union leverage or unfettered union power. They seek a measure of balance between means and ends, bilateralism without pathology.

It should also be clear that interested policy analysts lack adequate causal theory. This confounds their ability to estimate the tractability of the problem and to structure the mechanics of a successful policy response (Sabatier and Mazmanian, 1980). Some consistent empirical findings about policy efficacy in the contexts of union power and service disruption would go a long way toward reducing the uncertainty they encounter in the literature. This is easier said than done. The confusion is largely the result of missing data. Research thus far consists of cross-sectional and jurisdiction- or occupation-specific analyses, predominately the work of labor economists. Varied units of analysis, time points, and indicators complicate the ability to generalize about policy outcomes.

If the scholarly community is uncertain, imagine the confusion of the political generalist, the state legislator or city council member whom we left facing a political maelstrom a few pages ago. Chances are that she will muddle through satisfactorily, and she might even reap the whirlwind to her advantage. She could also fail miserably.

Lacking a better option, the policymaker is forced to use trial and error to construct policy. The wide variation in subnational public sector labor policy between and within states substantiates the fact that disjointed incrementalism (Braybrooke and Lindblom, 1963) is the dominant decision-making strategy at work in this sphere. Policy across the states is a varied patchwork of provisions, a series of experiments lying on a continuum of mandated collective bargaining to outright prohibition. Policy within states varies by occupation: police and firefighters are treated differently from teachers or state personnel. Further complicating the picture is that local jurisdictions of sufficient autonomy sometimes choose to provide their employees with alternative bargaining arrangements.[5]

More research is mandated if greater consensus about problems and solutions is to be achieved, and particularly if the probability of failure for subnational legislators is to be reduced. It appears, for example, that state assemblies do indeed recognize the benefits associated with institutionalized collective bargaining. Over the course of the past two decades an increasing number adopted the rudiments of a labor-management relationship. A few, such as Alaska and Hawaii, constructed quite elaborate schemes for bargaining with their public employees.

At the same time, however, the spectre of service disruption remains significant, compelling most of them to enact sticks as well as carrots into the law. In fact, it can be argued that in many cases state legislators overreact to this perceived threat, adopting harsh policy provisions such as mandatory arbitration or strike bans (Redenius, 1976). Although such measures may be attractive, involuntary impasse procedures can (among other effects) "chill" the potential for actual negotiation and compromise to occur. Strike prohibitions and penalties (as described above) may compromise or negate labor's bargaining leverage if strictly enforced. The result, therefore, is policy that works at cross-purposes, policy that contains the seeds of contradiction even as it attempts to harvest the fruits of bilateralism.

By attempting to sort out issues like these, the results of the analysis to follow should have important implications for the vitality of pluralist democracy in our public jurisdictions. The "normal" competition of interests described by Bentley, Truman, and Dahl is the theoretical justification underlying stringent regulation of the bargaining process. Although much of the past debate in this regard revolves around the utility of the strike ban, it should be apparent from the previous discussion that other policy mechanisms like those associated with bargaining rights and the use of arbitration procedures, for example, can play a significant role as well. In sum, the questions central to this research—why and how to manage collective bargaining—have direct impact upon labor as one competitor among many for scarce public goods. The ultimate hope is that this work will shed some important light upon the levers which may enable policymakers to manage the process in line with their goals. The extent to which they can adjust these levers will help to determine, in the context of the larger menu of alternatives available to them, the fairness of the playing field for which they have responsibility.

NOTES

1. Adoption is by no means assured; unexpected traffic fines and public perception that Big Brother lurks nearby may limit the feasibility of this alternative.

2. Chimezie Osigweh (to whom we turn next) deals explicitly with most of the major elements of the pluralist model at issue here. He does not, however, deal with the concept of overlapping memberships, which is so important to Truman's (1951) conception of the process, and which emerges from this discussion. The fact that unionized public employees are also taxpayers complicates these generalizations to the extent that there is no distinct "public employees vs. the public" dispute. For example, this dual role of employee and citizen leads analysts of the "third" school on sovereignty (to be described momentarily) to argue for even greater state protection from union power, given the two-pronged pressure which can be exerted by this group.

3. Even Woodrow Wilson quickly realized the error of this position, apparently repudiating his 1887 view within three years. See Martin, 1988, pp. 632–33 for details.

4. See chapter 3 for a more detailed discussion of the Boston strike.

5. The City of Columbia, Missouri, is a good example of this disjunction between state policy and local bargaining reality. See chapter 4 and appendix 5.1 for a more detailed discussion of this case and the implications of the general issue for the research therein.

2 The Need for Further Testing

Political scientists appear to spend very little time thinking about the role and impact of organized labor in American society. We might identify a union or two as examples of labor's presence in interest group politics for our undergraduates. We might discuss problems like those of PATCO or Eastern as they emerge in the headlines. But this seems to be about as far as many of us are interested in pursuing the matter.

There may be good reasons for this lack of attention. We may hesitate to encroach upon the economists' turf. Maybe we buy into some of the popular wisdom outlined in the introduction: unions are dinosaurs and they are on the wane anyway, making organized labor downright uninteresting, or, worse, irrelevant. Perhaps we lose interest in the story because we think we know the ending: labor is courted in every election, but can deliver few or none to the courtiers. (If this is true, then it would appear that candidates will not have a lack of respect added to the list of their alleged moral failures.)

If the policy issues described in the first chapter are not enough to justify our time, we might become more interested if we think a little harder about at least two dimensions of the process which make it a natural fit with the conceptions we have about ourselves and our profession.

First, it should be obvious by now that collective bargaining is about power. The fact that workers can constrain the budgetary and procedural flexibility of economic and political institutions makes many of us uneasy, along the lines suggested in chapter 1. The implications that collective bargaining has for the distribution of power in American society are indeed recognized when legislation designed to regulate the activity of either party to the bargaining relationship is enacted. Congress used the commerce clause to establish a uniform collective bargaining framework for the private sector. However, an alternative rationale was required for public employees if the "normal" pluralist operation of the system and the "sovereignty" of the public employer were to be protected.

National policymakers are apparently still looking for one. The regulation of bargaining in the public sector is more complicated, reflecting the development and structure of the federal system. The lack of an equally compelling constitutional argument led to four results in the public sector: (1) no uniform or comprehensive national framework covering all public employees, (2) bargaining rights for federal workers weakly grounded across a succession of executive orders and riders to other bills (with these actions not provided statutory authority until the Civil Service Reform Act of 1978), (3) wide variation in the rights and procedures available to those employed by subnational governments, and (4) limited bargaining rights and close regulation of public employee conduct in general.

If the power dimension of the public sector labor-management relationship does not make a case strong enough to merit its study as a political question, then it might be considered from a second angle. The greatest virtue of our role as applied policy analysts is the desire to inform the policymaking process. The facts are that (1) collective bargaining is a recent addition to the public sector, and (2) policy across state and local governments, the levels for which most public servants work, is quite diverse. Both mean that a great deal of the variance in policy and outcome remains unexplained, and that we are therefore of little help to policymakers.

THE TASK OF POLICY ANALYSIS

Thomas Dye (1979) believes that the task of policy analysis is to find out "what governments do, why they do it, and what difference it makes" (p. 652), a charge as instructive as it is elegant. If pressed to respond to these three dimensions of analysis in the context of subnational public sector labor policy, we would have a difficult time formulating a response of much depth.

What Governments Do

One reason for our veiled understanding of state labor policy is that widespread union activity is relatively new to the public sector. It was not until 1962 that Executive Order 10988 provided rudimentary representational rights for federal employees, an action which served to legitimize organizing efforts by public employees. Subnational jurisdictions took Kennedy's lead and began instituting legislative provisions of their own. In 1959, thirty-nine states had no policy; by 1969 all but fourteen had addressed the matter in some fashion, and a handful even went so far as to establish mechanisms for terminal dispute resolution (Freeman, 1986, p. 47). The trend toward institutionalized collective bargaining continues since that time.

A second contributor to confusion about what governments do is the complexity of these laws. As discussed previously, policy varies widely because governments as employers face a great deal of uncertainty about how to deal with their organized (and organizing) employees. Moreover, accessible data on that complex of statutory actions, opinions of state attorneys general, and court decisions which comprise the subnational bargaining environment eluded us until now. Fortunately, a longitudinal database constructed recently by the National Bureau of Economic Research (Valletta and Freeman, 1985) increases the precision of the measurement.

Why They Do it

Studies capable of systematically identifying the antecedents of policy response are sparse in the literature. In fact, only two pieces of research (Kochan, 1973; Faber and Martin, 1979) speak to this question, and both are limited in scope. The former employs a first-generation index of 1972 policy to find that change in per capita income, state per capita expenditures of government, and innovativeness explain about one-third of the policy variance. The latter examines unionism among teachers in 1968 and 1975, to find that urbanization and ideology (i.e., conservatism) promote and retard policy adoption, respectively.

What Difference It Makes

The impacts of subnational labor policy continue to be the subject of much debate. Two relatively recent and comprehensive reviews of the literature offer good summaries of the cumulative scholarship (and uncertainty) in this policy sphere.

Methe and Perry (1980) examine empirical work associated with three impacts of collective bargaining in local government: its wage effects, its implications for resource utilization (productivity in particular), and its influence upon expenditure levels. They find evidence, first, that wage gains are uneven across occupations. Though various analysts observe that some groups (e.g., firefighters, transit operators) achieve significant gains, other public servants (e.g., police) appear to experience only marginal improvements or they achieve no demonstrable economic benefit from bargaining. The authors are persuaded that labor costs probably increase when bilaterally determined, but the magnitude of the effect remains ambiguous. Studies of productivity also produce mixed signals. Methe and Perry conclude that "little of a general nature is known, except that collective bargaining continues to stimulate both positive and negative influences on productivity and work management" (p. 368). The authors' conclusions about the third dependent variable, spending, are their most concrete. The data they amass indicate that collective bargaining results in both higher levels of local expenditure and greater fiscal effort.

Freeman's (1986) review of the literature is even more expansive. He, too, identifies some common ground and some significant gaps in our understanding of labor relations in the public sector. His reading of the empirical research leads him to propose a series of (sometimes controversial) generalizations (pp. 42–44) which support and augment those found above.

On the Demand for Labor. Many early analyses of the phenomenon devoted a great deal of effort to distinguishing public from private sector bargaining. It is no real surprise that scholars would be interested in mapping the new terrain. Freeman's first conclusion acknowledges a consistent finding among his predecessors: that public sector labor unions have greater impact upon employer behavior than their private sector counterparts because of their dual status in the political process as employees and as voters (and as described in chapter 1). Yet Freeman disagrees with other analysts (e.g., Wellington and Winter) about the inelasticity of the demand curve. He argues that the discipline of a budget, the Tiebout adjustment, "legislative vetoes" of negotiated settlements, taxpayer referenda, and strike restrictions prohibit public unions from attaining great economic power.

On Policy and Unionization. Freeman clearly believes that policy matters. He argues that

[t]he growth of public sector unionism in the past two decades can be traced, in large part, to the passage of laws . . . that have sought to bring the private sector industrial relations model to the public sector. In states with laws favorable to unionism, public sector unionism has flourished; in states without such laws, it has not (p. 42).

He does find evidence, however, that this spurt in growth has ended.

On Unionism and Wages. The space he devotes to this subject accurately reflects the labor economists' emphasis upon wage issues. Freeman is less tentative than Methe and Perry about the impact of public sector unions upon labor costs. His central concern is about the size and structure of the effect; he accepts causation and argues magnitude. Though the cumulative finding is one of modest impact, Freeman proposes several reasons to question this result. Many wage studies, he argues, examined unions during a period of public sector expansion, when they were establishing themselves. Few distinguish between effects attributable to public employment and those reflecting occupational differences across the sectors. Cross-sectional analyses omit any spillover effects a settlement might have on subsequent comparability studies performed by other public jurisdictions. Standard datasets also miss significant differences in compensation packages. These factors lead Freeman to believe that the literature consistently understates the true long-term equilibrium impact of public sector unions on compensation.

Freeman also interprets research on the link between unionism and wage structure. He sees similarities and differences across sectors. Unlike the general trend toward equalization often observed in the private sector, "the teachers' unions appear to widen educational wage differentials, while police and firefighters' unions appear to have little effect on the range of salaries for their members" (p. 43). Yet like the private sector, unions in government have greater effect on fringe benefits than on wages, and there also appears to be less inequality in compensation among their members than among non-union employees.

On Strikes. Even in the face of widespread prohibitions, strikes continue to be frequent in public employment. As will be detailed below (chapter 5), the strongest generalization which can be made at the present time is that the configuration of strike policy has some impact upon the likelihood that disruption will occur. There is also evidence to suggest that most strikes are of short duration, and that mechanisms created to avoid them (e.g., various forms of arbitration) have been at least somewhat successful in doing so.

On Productivity and Expenditures. Freeman's review of the productivity literature supports the conclusion of Methe and Perry, although in his interpretation the glass is clearly half full. In his view, mixed results show that "unionism is not inimical to productivity" (p. 43). He does correctly point out, however, that wide differences in the operationalization of this concept complicate the ability to generalize. Like Methe and Perry as well, Freeman observes that unionization increases the share of budget required to cover labor costs.

On Gaps in the Literature. This review also identifies a number of areas in which research findings about the impacts of public sector collective bargaining are even sketchier. The relationships between unions and turnover, the dispersion of earnings, the effects of larger economic trends, and the total price of output require fundamental elaboration. Like many other analysts, Freeman believes that a specific public sector paradigm needs to be developed, one which addresses the distinctive aspects of labor relations involving a government employer. This new model must encompass unique political constraints and opportunities—constraints that lead to different outcomes and opportunities which allow unions to shift the demand curve outward through use of the political process.

THE NEED FOR FURTHER TESTING

This overview of a developing literature indicates that social scientists have made a significant contribution to what we know about the public side of collective bargaining. We know that an increasing number of governments adopted a wide array of policies designed to bring a structured labor relations environment to their jurisdictions beginning in the late 1950s and early 1960s. We know something about why they did so, in that we can identify a few distinguishing characteristics of those adopting some form of policy by the early 1970s. Finally, we know that bargaining, once established, may lead to important changes in the politics and economics associated with the process of governing.

Yet much work remains to be done if the new model called for by Freeman is to be developed. All three issues—what governments do, why they do it, and what difference it makes—merit further scrutiny. The latter two concerns are particularly compelling. First, a better sense of the policy determination process is required. Before they can hope to establish or to strengthen the labor-management relationship, policymakers must understand the environmental variables most likely to facilitate or to limit their ability to construct labor policy. Once the the boundaries of action are identified, they need, second, a clearer comprehension of the policy configuration(s) most likely to provide them with a net benefit from bilateralism.

Like the early cross-state comparative policy analysts, a lack of theory led some industrial relations scholars interested in the emerging public side of the phenomenon to adopt David Easton's (1953) systems approach to conceptualize their undertaking. Writing in 1973, Thomas Kochan argues that "the majority of the industrial relations literature addresses the *consequences* of public policy and thus implicitly treats policy as an independent variable . . . [I]t is more appropriate to view policy as an intervening variable between certain antecedent conditions and dependent variables of interest in labor-management relations" (p. 322). This logic suggests, therefore, that the relevant sequential model is one of

ANTECEDENTS→POLICY→OUTCOME

A common criticism of the systems framework is that it is too theoretical to be of much empirical utility. This is true, but it does lead analysts to think a bit more systematically about the issue of temporal precedence, a requirement for causation to be established and a source of continuing debate in the public sector labor relations literature.

Take, for example, findings regarding the relationship between policy and unionization. Freeman's assertion above is that unionism prospers in a sympathetic policy environment. Yet three more recent analyses (Burton and Thomason, 1988; Goldfield and Plotkin, 1987; Goldfield, 1990) provide reason to question the vitality of this conclusion. Burton and Thomason argue, in essence, that the direction posited in the studies cited by Freeman is the artifact of cross-sectional regressions, time-dependent policy variables, and in some cases, the use of an inappropriate indicator for unionization (i.e., substitution of the extent of coverage by a collective bargaining agreement for the degree of organization as the dependent variable). The Goldfield studies employ a proportional hazards function to test the utility of the laws hypothesis as an explanation for the surge in unionism during the early 1960s and throughout the century, respectively. Relying heavily upon teachers data collected by Saltzman (1985), both sets of results provide it little support; unionization, Goldfield contends, appears to be a self-sustaining process.

All three of these studies suggest that unionism may drive policy. The idea that policymaking is often reactive fits with intuition. The image of legislators feeling the need to "deal with" an increasingly unionized workforce does not seem far from the mark. While a lag between the need for policy and the actual response may come as no surprise, it may be much more difficult to ascertain whether the relationship between these two variables is recursive, unidirectional, or spurious. Chapters 4–6 will describe the conflicts associated with data, methodology, and findings in greater detail.

Closer consideration of the Easton paradigm in the public sector labor relations context reveals something else only implicitly addressed by the literature thus far. Simply stated, a distinction between outputs and outcomes may be required if a clear assessment of "what difference it makes" is to be achieved. Outcomes are the ultimate concern—the impacts that collective bargaining has upon the way the business of government is conducted (e.g., the organization of work, managerial autonomy, costs, and the productive use of limited resources). Yet it is the direct (or intermediate) output of policy—the character of the relationship constructed between labor and management—which may offer policymakers the greatest degree of control over, and may have the widest implications for, the results of collective bargaining.

Two dimensions of the labor-management relationship become relevant in this logic. The first encompasses the ability of the union to assume its role as partner in public decision making, a measure of the degree to which unions can develop enough strength to make the relationship bilateral. The second dimension speaks to the quality of the relationship itself, that is, whether it is one of harmony or of conflict.

Returning to Wellington and Winter momentarily, both (interrelated) components of this relationship, union strength and its characteristic level of (dis)harmony, play key roles in determining the outcomes of collective bargaining in the public sector. But surprisingly enough, clear links between labor policy and these variables have yet to be established.

Contrary to the tone of confidence underlying Freeman's assertions, only a handful of studies in the literature address the question of strength (typically measured through membership figures), and all are limited in some way. Two are cross-sectional (Moore, 1977; Dalton, 1982). Another is longitudinal but limited to teachers (Moore, 1978). The omission of other occupations is significant, given the varied results across service functions found in a fourth study (Seroka, 1985).

The pattern of the relationship between labor policy and labor peace (usually operationalized through disruption indicators) is even more ambiguous. In this case a "non-finding," rigorously attained (Burton and Krider, 1975), sparked a subsequent crusade designed to pursue its antithesis—that policymakers could indeed act in ways which might foster or impede strikes systematically. The result was a host of new analyses varying by model, unit of analysis, and time period. Though in this crusade scholars spilled much ink and little blood, a reassuring glimpse of the grail did materialize: the most consistent result is that policy appears to matter, although it is significant that about a third of these studies find reason to disagree.

THIS STUDY

The uncertainty manifest in what we know about the public side of collective bargaining reflects the natural diversity of a developing literature. Variation in theoretical approach, methodology, and available data leads to mixed or limited empirical results. Our ability to generalize is seriously impeded by occupation-, time-, and jurisdiction-specific analyses. It is clearly time to direct our energies toward developing a wider, cumulative understanding of the phenomenon if the seeds planted previously are to be nurtured to full bloom.

For various reasons social scientists too often break new ground and then fail to cultivate it thoroughly. The literature contains a host of interesting patterns abandoned before they could be fully tested. The research to follow is an effort to clarify and to elaborate the significant linkages of this policymaking sphere through the replication, synthesis, and refinement of ideas unearthed but untended in previous scholarship.

There is good reason to believe that more can be learned. As suggested previously, the dataset constructed by Valletta and Freeman at NBER offers a wider, longitudinal picture of policymaking activity. These new data cover the fifty states for thirty years (1955–1984) and disaggregate policy across fourteen categories of action and five functional occupations. They offer a comprehensive view of the policy environment not limited to legislative action, one occupation, or a cross section. This link in the measurement chain is therefore strengthened.

Though limited at both ends, a few strings of antecedents and impacts data do exist, allowing another look at both sides of the policy equation. For example, various reports by the Bureau of the Census contain data on the important unionization and disruption variables for most of the 1970s and the early 1980s in a form comparable to that of the intervening policy measures.

Broadly stated, the goal of this analysis is to identify the major causes and consequences of public sector labor policy. Three central questions guide this research:

1. What policy mechanisms have decision makers developed in their attempts to regulate the relationship between government and its employees?
2. What antecedent conditions account for policy variation in employee rights, employer obligations, and procedural regulations within and across governments?
3. What impacts do various policy configurations have upon the character of the labor-management relationship in government?

Public employees of the states and localities account for approximately 80 percent of the total public sector workforce (Troy and Sheflin, 1985, pp. 3–20). Subnational jurisdictions are therefore the focus of this analysis. Incorporating the Valletta and Freeman data, this study examines state-level policy associated with five categories of employment: (1) state (merit system) personnel, local (2) police, (3) fire, (4) teachers, and (5) "other local" employees (i.e., all other workers not included in categories (2) through (4), for example, the many occupations associated with public works in local jurisdictions).

The methodology at the heart of this effort is straightforward. Chapter 3 documents and analyzes the development of subnational public sector labor policy over the course of the thirty year period. Once this descriptive task is complete, each of the next two chapters identifies the major studies, findings, and limits relevant to what we know about the causes (chapter 4) and impacts (chapter 5) of policy in this sphere. In both cases, generalizations derived from the literature review are retested across what most often amounts to a wider set of occupations, time points, and/or jurisdictions. Chapter 6 summarizes the results, contributions, and bounds of this pursuit.

A critical assumption at work here is that a step back is in order if a step forward is to be achieved. Replication may appear to be less ambitious or exciting than does turning over the first shovel of a new piece of terrain. Yet replication is crucial to the philosophy of science because it usually includes synthesis and refinement important to greater understanding of social phenomena.

This research is grounded in two pieces of naked optimism: first, that we can and should generalize beyond teachers in 1972 or public employees facing a "permissive" legal environment, and, second, that ideas generated by this sort of broad-gauge mapping contain at least some indirect relevance to policymakers. This sort of journey is not undertaken without danger; the biggest risk is that past errors of perspective will be compounded. However, it will become quickly apparent (if it is not so already) that this venture is undertaken with little theoretical assistance. Primarily an effort in induction, its goal is to nail down that handful of linkages most critical to questions of policy efficacy. The hope is that these first steps toward reaching some firmer conclusions about thirty years' experience with collective bargaining in the public sector will eventually lead to a useful model of the phenomenon.

3 What Governments Do:
The History and Development of
Public Sector Bargaining Provisions

This chapter addresses the first task of policy analysis defined by Dye—
what governments do. Its purposes are threefold: to trace the history and
development of public sector labor policy as it has evolved in the United
States, to elaborate the types of decisions that policymakers face should
they decide to establish a system of collective bargaining in their jurisdictions, and to describe the nature, scope, and change associated with
the policy environments constructed in the states and localities since the
late 1950s.

HISTORICAL ROOTS

Diverse sets of public employees organized themselves long before
they engaged in any form of collective bargaining. Yet a lengthy period
of ferment resulted in no more than a limited set of policy victories,
particularly at the subnational level. Public workers were certainly part
of the general movement to reduce hours and to improve wages and
working conditions at the turn of the century. But their fortunes would
later diverge dramatically from those of their private sector counterparts.

Craftsmen at naval installations unionized in the early 1800s. Teacher
associations appeared in the 1850s, police and fire (i.e., the IAFF) in the
1880s. Postal workers began organizing with the Knights of Labor in the
late 1880s; the National Association of Letter Carriers (NALC) and the
National Federation of Postal Clerks (NFPC) became early affiliates of
the fledgling AFL when Samuel Gompers left the Knights after the Hay-

market riot in 1886 (Gordon, 1986, p. 358; Holley and Jennings, 1980, pp. 33–42).

Though they did not possess any sort of formal recognition, these early organizations did make themselves felt. Strikes at U.S. Navy Yards in the 1830s led President Martin Van Buren to order a shorter (i.e., ten-hour) workday in 1840 (Gordon, 1986, p. 358). The New York Patrol-men's Benevolent Association won several salary increases between 1890 and 1907, as did the Chicago Teachers' Federation in 1902. Street cleaners in Rhode Island won a Saturday "half-holiday" in 1907 (Holley and Jennings, 1980, p. 443). Gag orders by Roosevelt and Taft, which for-bade petitions to Congress about wages and working conditions, spurred postal organizations to agitate for the right to organize and to lobby on the Hill. Over a decade of effort led to an early legislative success: although more commonly remembered for its provisions requiring dis-missal for cause in the federal service (thereby closing the "back door" to patronage left open by the Pendleton Act), the Lloyd-LaFollette Act (1912) provided the only statutory guarantee of federal employee organ-izing rights until passage of the Civil Service Reform Act in 1978.[1] Strikes by police in Cincinatti (1918) and in Boston (1919) evidenced an emerging militancy among their ranks.

The Boston strike remains the more famous of the two (or maybe infamous, from James David Barber's perspective), probably because it was such a notable early failure and because of its impact on the career of Calvin Coolidge. It is understatement to suggest that working condi-tions for the Boston police were miserable:

Their starting salary was $1000, of which some $200 went for equipment and uniforms. Annual increases were $100 to a maximum salary of $1600. In May 1919 the city had authorized the first pay raise in 6 years, $200 for all patrolmen. This increase was far outweighed by the skyrocketing cost of living, which had gone up 86 percent during the period. The patrolmen averaged an 87-hour work week and had to put up with outrageous working conditions. The patrolmen's wives constantly complained of the cockroaches which accompanied their husbands home and shared their clothing. Vermin-eaten helmets were also a source of displeasure. Although there was a civil service system, the police commissioner, a gubernatorial appointee, was not required to promote on the basis of promotion lists. Thus a patrolman could rank at the top of the eligible list and remain there, despite openings, until he retired. Personal acceptability to the commissioner was the key to success (Shafritz et. al., 1986, pp. 261–262).

Though collective action would appear logical from a cadre of public servants facing these circumstances, this logic was lost upon, among others, Governor Coolidge. To Gompers' protests that police should be allowed to form a union and to affiliate with the AFL, Coolidge offered what may have been the greatest line of his political career: "There is no right to strike against the public safety by anybody, anywhere, anytime," a classic piece of no-nonsense, law-and-order rhetoric that would carry him into the vice-presidency and then into the White House upon Warren G. Harding's death in 1923.

Order was restored and the strikers eventually returned to their jobs. But the country's first taste of a municipal labor problem was a sour one, which apparently lingered for awhile. Although workers in the industrial sector would win a series of congressional victories that would institutionalize a comprehensive framework for collective bargaining over the next four decades (i.e., Norris-LaGuardia, 1932; Wagner-Connery, 1935; Taft-Hartley, 1947; Landrum-Griffin, 1959), the public side of the movement heard little but policy silence until 1962.

The little they did hear emanated from Philadelphia, which began negotiating labor agreements with city employees in 1939, from New York City, which was bargaining by 1958, and from the progressives in Wisconsin, the first state with a comprehensive labor relations plan for (and limited to) local government in the nation (1959). It was not until Kennedy provided a score—Executive Order 10988 in 1962—that public employees had any hope of hearing a symphony in place of this distant trio.

EO 10988 appears to have been a watershed event in the public sector labor movement for at least three reasons. For the first time federal employees were provided with the protected right to join, or to refrain from joining, a labor organization (Federal Labor Relations Authority, 1981, p. 1). Second, it was to subnational policymakers the signal of a decided change in national philosophy toward the role of collective bargaining in government. Finally, Kennedy's action also marked the beginning of a two-track system of public sector labor relations reflecting (as suggested in chapter 2) the shape of the federal system. Federal regulation of state and local bargaining has been proposed often, and in many forms.[2] But the absence of such legislation to date means that the policy configuration at the national level remains quite distinct from the wide variation in legal environments observable across state and local governments (see below).

Policy covering federal employees thereby diverged, to be further refined in a succession of executive orders (most significantly by Nixon in EO 11491 of 1970) which ultimately led to statutory grounding in Title VII of the Civil Service Reform Act of 1978. In sum, vehicles were invented to take private sector, and then federal employees on the road to their respective bargaining destinations. Yet members of the subnational workforce were left behind, required either to continue their wait or to find separate conveyance.

At least two other sets of national level decisions had significant impact upon their cause, however. In *AFSCME, AFL-CIO v. Woodward* (1969) the Supreme Court declared the right of employees to join unions to be protected by the First and Fourteenth Amendments. Public administrators denying these rights became subject to court action for damages under the Civil Rights Act of 1871 (Holley and Jennings, 1980, p. 444).

A second, more controversial decision emerged from the Court in 1976. Congress passed a set of amendments to the Fair Labor Standards Act in 1974. Among its provisions was one extending minimum wage and maximum hour regulations to most employees of subnational jurisdictions. Resistant to such coverage,[3] the states and localities petitioned the Supreme Court for relief. In *National League of Cities v. Usery* (1976) they received a favorable response: writing for the Court, Justice Rehnquist argued that application of these provisions to the states and their political subdivisions

will impermissibly interfere with the integral governmental functions of these bodies . . . [T]heir application will . . . significantly alter or displace the States' abilities to structure employer-employee relationships in such areas as fire prevention, police protection, sanitation, public health, and parks and recreation. . . . If Congress may withdraw from the States the authority to make those fundamental employment decisions upon which their systems for performance of these functions must rest, we think there would be little left of the States' "separate and independent existence" (Grodin et. al., 1979, p. 352).

This decision had radical implication for intergovernmental relationships because it represented the first real restriction on Congress's use of the commerce power since the 1930s. It explicitly overturned the Court's previous ruling in *Maryland v. Wirtz* (1968), which upheld extension of the FLSA to employees of schools, hospitals, and other state " 'enterprises' not dissimilar to those in the private sector" (Mass and Gottlieb, 1979, p. 63) based upon the impact of state employment practices on interstate commerce (Ducat and Chase, 1988, p. 361).

Many analysts viewed *Usery* as the death knell for any hope of a federally regulated system of state and local collective bargaining. Others were not so sure. In the previous year (*Fry v. US*, 1975) the Court validated extension to the states of a temporary wage freeze associated with the Economic Stabilization Act of 1970. In *Usery* Rehnquist distinguished, but refused to overturn, *Fry* on three grounds: (1) that a temporary freeze was a limited intrusion on state sovereignty necessitated by a "national emergency," (2) that it "displaced no state choices as to how governmental operations should be structured," and (3) that it reduced, rather than increased, pressures upon state budgets (Grodin et. al., 1979, p. 353).

This facet of the opinion led two observers to argue in 1979 that a national labor relations framework for subnational employees was not doomed; instead, they viewed it as a "logical imperative" (Mass and Gottlieb, 1979). They based their case upon a point often overlooked by many opponents of unionism in general: that collective bargaining is a *procedure* for negotiating terms of employment, not a mandate of specific conditions. Because, as Weinstock (1969, p. 360) affirms, "neither concession nor compromise [is] demanded by the legal concept of bargaining in good faith," collective bargaining is decidedly less intrusive than laws regulating wages and hours. This logic and their faith in the process carried Mass and Gottlieb to the conclusion that "the benefits of such legislation and the possibility, if not probability, of its constitutionality make its passage and eventual testing in the courts a worthwhile governmental exercise" (p. 66).

The *Usery* majority collapsed nine years later, providing the proponents of national action with even greater hope. Though in subsequent cases it attempted to redefine a sphere of state autonomy, the Court soon recognized the futility of the quest (Ducat and Chase, 1988, pp. 361–362). The justices abandoned the attempt in *Garcia v. San Antonio Metropolitan Transit Authority* (1985), overturning *Usery* and ratifying the application of FLSA provisions to state mass transit systems:

We . . . now reject, as unsound in principle and unworkable in practice, a rule of state immunity from federal regulation that turns on a judicial appraisal of whether a particular governmental function is "integral" or "traditional." Any such rule leads to inconsistent results. . . . State sovereign interests . . . are more properly protected by procedural safeguards inherent in the structure of the federal system than by judicially created limitations on federal power (Ducat and Chase, 1988, pp. 368, 371).

It remains to be seen whether proposals like Clay's (above) will gain enough momentum to take advantage of this revision. Absent such legislation the subnational policy environment will retain its fragmented character. The next section of this chapter elaborates the source of this fragmentation, describing the wide range of choices facing state and local policy actors as they grapple with the questions of whether and how to define collective bargaining in their jurisdictions.

DESIGN ISSUES

Subnational policymakers face two major categories of choice: rights and mechanics. The first decision they must make is whether to engage in some form of collective negotiations with their employees. This typically involves a fierce legislative battle, in that the central issue revolves around labor's "appropriate" claim to some portion of (initially unfettered) management prerogative over terms and conditions of employment. If and when such a sphere of negotiable issues is constructed, the next step is to make their negotiation operational. The mechanics of the process encompass three sets of successive and recurring activities: (1) selection of labor's bargaining representative, (2) negotiation of a written contract, and (3) administration of its provisions. Figure 3.1 provides a schematic representation of the basic model. The issues included at each of these decision points follow in detail.

Bargaining Rights

As suggested above, the central issue involved in the question of bargaining rights is one of managerial autonomy, particularly the degree to which the public employer is obligated to reach written agreement with its organized employees over conduct of the workplace. State legislatures typically resolve this matter in one of four ways.[4] Some explicitly prohibit bargaining in any form. Others take a permissive stance, in which the state or local employers are authorized, but not obligated, to deal with the union(s). A third configuration allows employee representatives to present proposals or, similarly, to "meet and confer" with management's agent. The final (and most probargaining) policy position is one in which the employer has the affirmative duty to negotiate in good faith until agreement is reached.

Though the others are straightforward, the third category of mechanisms merits brief elaboration. Under a "proposals only" or meet-and-confer sort of system, the employer is obliged to listen to union initiatives but retains ultimate decision-making authority. This form of employee rights is clearly designed with at least two complementary purposes in mind. The first is to open a channel of regular communication between management and labor. The hope is to enhance the quality of government operations in direct proportion to the value of labor's input and the morale boost accompanying greater participation. Second, such a strategy obviously requires management to give up very little of its decision-making authority. As Edwards (1973) indicates, "under a pure meet-and-confer

Figure 3.1
The Labor Relations Process

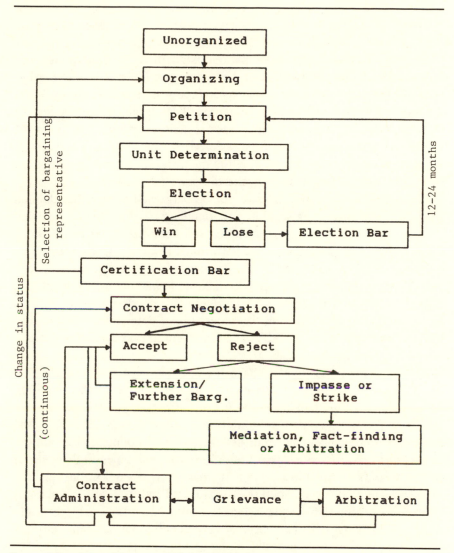

Source: Adapted from Schuman and Olufs, 1988, p. 277.

bargaining model, the outcome of any public employer-employee discussions will depend more on management's determinations than on bilateral decisions by 'equals' at the bargaining table" (p. 895). His use of the adjective "pure" is intentional: easy to distinguish in theory, the distinction between meet-and-confer arrangements and full-scale collective bargaining becomes much cloudier in practice when statutory limitations on the scope of negotiations are considered.

The Scope of Bargaining

The range of negotiable issues is obviously critical to the status actually possessed by public employees at the bargaining table. The relationship between these two variables is a positive one: bilateralism increases as the scope of bargainable subjects expands. The possibility that collective bargaining may be legalized, but limited to a very narrow range of benign workplace concerns (from the perspective of managerial prerogative), means that negotiability is probably the most significant dimension of the rights question. It is the flesh on the bones of intention.

The scope of what may or may not be bargained is typically defined by policy in a three-part scheme: (1) mandatory issues, (2) permissible subjects, and (3) those items excluded or prohibited from negotiation. Labor, of course, prefers movement from (3) toward (1), while management autonomy is enhanced by the opposite vector. Yet this characterization is too simplistic by half—the substance of the issues to be bargained rather than their absolute number is of greatest concern to both parties. Because ''joint determination'' equates with ''delegation'' to the employer, state legislatures and city councils prefer to trade breadth for depth ''so long as the actual encroachment by the union upon the issues is limited'' (Bent and Reeves, 1978, p. 62).

Subnational jurisdictions toil greatly to achieve congruence between definitions of scope and their notions of sovereignty. Like the private sector, many states construct explicit and elaborate statements to define those specific management rights not displaced by collective bargaining. These sorts of provisions most often exempt the types and levels of services to be delivered, personnel matters (i.e., selection, defined broadly, and job classification decisions), and merit system regulations from the process. Unlike the federal level, compensation is generally negotiable among state and local governments adopting some form of public sector legislation, as are working conditions, layoff/rehiring mechanisms, and grievance procedures (Gordon, 1986, pp. 368–369; Bent and Reeves, 1978, p. 61).[5]

Two additional observations about the significance of these choices should be documented before we proceed. First, to pick up the discussion suspended a couple of pages ago, the interplay between rights and scope provisions is one instance in which the practical muddle between collective negotiations and meet-and-confer arrangements is manifest. Edwards suggests that restrictions on the number and substance of issues to be negotiated mean that the states typically engage in something less than complete bargaining and something more than limited consultation with their employees:

It is generally assumed that most states . . . have opted for the collective negotiations model over the meet-and-confer approach. . . . [T]his conclusion appears to be somewhat overdrawn and, at best, misleading. Actually, most states have rejected the pure meet-and-confer bargaining model, but, by the same token, most have also rejected the collective negotiations approach. In practice, most states have adopted either a "modified" meet-and-confer statute, which gives unions more bargaining power than the pure model, or a "modified" collective-negotiations statute, which is more restrictive from the union's viewpoint than its private sector counterpart. For this reason alone, it is often difficult to distinguish between meet-and-confer and collective negotiations as viable working concepts in the public sector (1973, p. 896).

We therefore find less bargaining than we might otherwise expect.

The second issue with relevance here speaks to the nature of changes in scope over time and highlights, once again, a critical difference between industry and government. Absent specific legal boundaries (as is true for the most part in the private sector), and the subjects for bargaining are themselves negotiable. In this sense, bilateralism evolves as the labor-management relationship progresses. On the public side, however, sub-national legislators often circumvent this evolution and restrict negotiability by constructing statutes and ordinances which incrementally displace mutual agreement by the parties actually sitting at the table (e.g., union security, initially defined as a negotiable item, becomes less so when dues checkoff is specifically authorized for union members by law at some later date). In this sense, the scope of bargaining both affects and reflects the relative political power of each side. Frequent end runs make negotiation a mere facade: "the real confrontation over issues takes place at other levels and institutions of government . . . collective bargaining becomes a sideshow, while the main event is played in the political environment" (Bent and Reeves, 1978, p. 61).

Selection of the Bargaining Representative

Once the public employer decides to engage in some form of negotiation over a defined set of issues, public employees have a green light to initiate the effort to select their bargaining representative(s). This step is, of course, necessary for bargaining to occur. More significant for the nature of the labor-management relationship, however, are the answers that result in response to the four key questions involved here: (1) who is to be represented? (the unit determination issue); (2) on what terms? (the form of representation); (3) by whom? (election provisions); and (4) for how long? (the term of recognition).[6]

The process begins with an organizing campaign, by employees dissatisfied with the terms of their employment (an internal locus of activity) or, alternatively, from (or in conjunction with) an external stimulus—agitation by a union entrepreneur seeking to increase membership. Stated in a more positive fashion, they see benefits to be derived from unionizing. Starling suggests that unions traditionally claim to offer four main advantages to those they hope to represent:

1. Economic security: job security; a fair wage; an acceptable standard of living;
2. Job satisfaction: voice in work rules; a clean and safe working environment;
3. Equitable treatment: protection from arbitrary management actions; a guarantee of fair application of work rules and requirements; and
4. Grievance procedures: the ability to pursue complaints about work issues without fear of retaliation by management (1982, p. 541).

Nigro and Nigro (1986) augment this list from a systemic perspective. They attribute the militancy beginning in the 1960s to relative deprivation and a new self-awareness: public employees increasingly felt they were not keeping pace with the post-WWII expansion of the private sector, while also recognizing their expanding numbers and position in the economy.

The Nigros develop additional noneconomic explanations as well. They examine the voice issue with a white collar focus. In their view, this segment of the government workforce seeks to organize as a response to the troubling impersonality of the work environment, coupled with a growing list of concerns about the quality of service delivery. These workers also reject employer paternalism which, according to the authors, they perceive as denying them an opportunity for input. In particular, this group appears to have lost confidence in "management's" civil service system—they are disillusioned with inadequate compensation, lopsided grievance procedures, and the unilateral determination of personnel practices (pp. 116–121). As a final note, we add one other (self-explanatory) variable to this set of motivations: the solidary benefits associated with union membership (e.g., Salisbury, 1969).

Interested for any of these reasons, that segment of a jurisdiction's labor contingent hoping to unionize and to bargain may proceed in one of two ways. They can seek informal acceptance of their designated employee representative by the employer, or they may initiate efforts to achieve official certification through a formal administrative process. The informal route has two disadvantages. The first reflects the possibility that voluntary acquiescence by the employer may be perceived as "too easy," thereby engendering suspicion of collusion or a sweetheart arrangement between management and labor leadership. Mistrust of this sort has significant implications, of course, for employee unity and the quality of the labor-management relationship. The second potential difficulty lies in the fact that the employer may unilaterally renege on this commitment at some later date (along the lines of the "proverb" described in chapter 1).

Though some allow both forms, all states with a bargaining law make provision for formal certification. The mechanics of the process require a number of significant choices. The first is one of institutional arrangements. In the vast majority of cases, the state establishes a Public Employee Relations Board or Commission (a PERB or PERC) with sole responsibility for labor relations. Others prefer to locate such authority in an existing department (most often Labor), or to decentralize by agency or function (e.g., all bargaining matters relevant to teachers might be referred to the Department of Education). Like personnel matters generally, it is probably the case that the ultimate decision will depend most heavily upon the importance that policymakers place (or are pressured into placing) upon a strong, central presence in this sphere.

From this context, the representation question enters the unit determination phase. As its name suggests, the goal of this stage is to determine who is to be included in the bargaining unit, an important question for at least two reasons. It defines who may vote in the certification election, and with a subsequent union victory, it decides who will be represented in negotiations and eventually covered by a contract.

States employ a host of criteria designed to rationalize their decisions here. Though a jurisdiction might add others, a scan of the statutes indicates that six standards are most commonly utilized:

1. Community of interest: job similarities (e.g., duties, skills, promotional ladders, compensation, working conditions) and functional integration (e.g., operational dependence, common supervision);

2. Desires of employer and employees;

3. Efficiency and effectiveness concerns;

4. History of organizing and bargaining activity;

5. Limiting fragmentation; and

6. Separation or exclusion of supervisory, professional, and confidential personnel (U.S. Department of Labor, 1981, pp. 501–530).

It is typically the administrative vehicle vested with authority for labor relations that weighs these concerns and makes the final call. In most cases, two major types of bargaining units result from these deliberations. They are constructed on an agency (e.g., police, fire department) or occupational (e.g., clerical, maintenance) basis.

The size and number of units established at this step have important implications for the bargaining process and its outcomes. Both management and labor prefer large units to small ones for fairly obvious reasons. From the employer's perspective, a handful of big units reduces the sheer number of negotiations in which it must engage, decreases strike potential, and limits vulnerability to the "whipsaw" of multilateral demands. Unions prefer the membership gains associated with a large cadre of employees for which it is the sole bargaining agent (though the size-cohesion tradeoff is of interest to both sides).

This is the point at which the second significant component of selection—the form of recognition—enters the picture. Nearly all states now provide exclusive recognition by statute, in which one labor organization represents all members of the bargaining unit. This was not always so. California's first comprehensive bargaining law required the public employer to meet and confer with a union "on behalf of its members." Similarly, California and Minnesota experimented briefly with proportional representation, negotiating with a council of employee representatives. Though subsequently abandoned by EO 11491 (above), EO 10988 established a third variant, in which the majority union received "formal" recognition while organizations claiming members in the minority were conferred "informal" status and concomitant consultation rights (Grodin et al., 1979, pp. 40–41). Experience with these nonexclusive configurations apparently led subnational policymakers to realize that a single agent "discourages union competition, minimizes interorganizational factionalism, simplifies negotiations for both sides, makes the administration of an agreement easier, provides the union with a strong and stable membership, and reduces the possibility of a strike" (Bent and Reeves, 1978, p. 68).

Having made the decision to provide exclusive recognition, the process through which employees select their representative must be forged (the third dimension of the selection step). In general, such provisions include:

1. Ballot composition: In the modal case, approximately one-third of the bargaining unit must sign the initial petition for certification. Another 10 percent of all members are

required for an alternative candidate to appear. In addition, almost all states require a "no-union" option as well.

2. Logistics: The form of notice required, timing, place of election, and runoff procedures are often specified.

3. Noninterference requirements: The set of employer and employee actions threatening to bias the outcome of the election may also be explicitly prohibited.

Though it might be logically included in this list of provisions, policy choice involving the term of recognition (the fourth major piece of the selection puzzle) merits separate attention. Briefly, states must decide how to handle the two outcomes of any election: a union win or a union loss. With a victory, a certification period is usually defined—the length of time that must elapse before the representation question may come up again. With a defeat, the certification bar becomes an election bar—the minimum period guaranteed until another vote can be called. A twelve-month requirement is most common across the states, though it can extend two or three times longer if contract expiration is also included in the calculus.

Union Security

The form and term of recognition clearly affect a union's toehold in the public organization and in the bargaining process. There are a handful of additional policy issues with even greater significance for the sureness of its footing. Decisions about automatic dues deduction, union or agency shop arrangements, and Right-to-Work legislation have critical implications for union security. All are controversial, because they bring to the surface some of the most belligerent value conflicts associated with unionism. If it is balance they seek (or require), policymakers are forced once again (lacking Teflon, Solomon, or a net) to engineer institutionalized advantage in a perilous environment; they must address the free rider problem without trampling individual rights nor legislating the demise of unions and their competitors.

Dues checkoff is the least contentious of these mechanisms. Employees provide written authorization for their membership dues to be deducted from their paychecks automatically. The labor organization typically pays the employer for the cost of this service, and in return receives a hassle-free flow of stable income. This is also a low-cost, high-gain proposition from management's perspective. Automated payroll systems provide an economy of scale which makes this cheap to implement relative to the potential magnitude of the concession its bargaining team can negotiate in trade.

Union and agency shop provisions provoke much more debate about the degree to which union membership is to be be a term of employment. In a union shop, the employee is required to join the labor organization at the end of the probationary period. Though distinct from the traditional closed shop in which membership is a precondition of employment (outlawed by Taft-Hartley), the provisions are similar in the degree of compulsion they embody for the individual. The agency shop concept was developed largely in response to this concern. In this configuration, all members of the bargaining unit pay a sum equal to the costs incurred by the union for their representation (e.g., in the negotiations process and in grievance proceedings). Also known as "fair share" agreements, the logic of the vehicle is that (1) the certified agent should be compensated for its efforts given the legal obligation to represent the entire unit regardless of membership status, and (2) persons who prefer not to join the union should not be compelled to do so, nor should they be required to pay for unwanted services (e.g., a political agenda).[7]

The express intent of Right-to-Work laws is to eliminate compulsion entirely. As the name suggests, proponents of these statutes classify any individual's right to work as fundamental, as they do the right to join (or to refrain from joining) an organization of any sort. Thus these laws outlaw any form of union security by definition. Opponents, of course, label them anti-union, a contention which appears to be supported by the conventional wisdom: "ostensibly passed to protect employees from pressures to join a union, they actually seek to make it difficult for unions to exist" (Schuman and Olufs, 1988, p. 275). Further discussion of the dispute and the effectiveness of these laws is unnecessary to this description. The relevant point is that Taft-Hartley buried one alternative and birthed another in 1947. Though lying at the other end of the continuum from its logical (if expired) foil in the closed shop, the Right-to-Work option provides subnational decision makers with an extreme policy solution to the question of union security.

Contract Negotiation

Having established some structure for codetermination, the next step in the collective bargaining process is the actual negotiation of the contract. Subnational policymakers face two sets of important choices at this stage: (1) institutional arrangements for bargaining with their employees, and (2) impasse resolution procedures. The issues associated with fragmented authority on management's side of the bargaining table were described in chapter 1. Suffice it to say here that the key delegation questions involved are typically resolved either (1) in the context of the centralization-decentralization discussion (i.e., when responsibility for labor relations is allocated to PERB and/or agency discretion), or (2) incrementally, with the mechanics of authority reformulated as experience with bargaining accrues.

What to do in the event of a negotiations breakdown is of observably greater concern to legislators worried about the potential costs of strikes (for reasons also covered in the introduction). In their effort to avoid such collapse, policymakers often incorporate one or more third-party procedures for resolving impasses into the bargaining statutes they construct. They have a number of options from which to choose: mediation, fact-finding, or some form of arbitration.

In the case of mediation, a neutral individual acceptable to both parties is invited to the table in order to promote continued talks, to discuss disagreements with each side, to channel messages, and to suggest means for reconciling disputes. The mediator's central mission is to facilitate compromise between the parties themselves. The person selected for this role has no authority to impose binding solutions.

Fact-finding is sometimes employed when mediation fails (and before the arbitration step mentioned below). As the name suggests, this neutral individual investigates the "facts" surrounding the issues in contention. Wage-comparability and ability-to-pay questions are probably the most common foci of this technique. Findings are typically released through a written report, which may or may not contain specific substantive or procedural recommendations for ending the impasse. This document has strategic value for both sides, to the extent that it is the vehicle most responsible for bringing visibility to (and therefore public opinion into) the stalemate.

Arbitration is undoubtedly the most controversial (and most studied) of the three procedures because it often involves greater coercion than its counterparts. In its conventional form, a final and binding "award" must result once this step is initiated (which can occur voluntarily, or because it is the compulsory terminal step of the impasse-resolution process). Alternatively, its major variants include:

1. Final-offer (package) arbitration: in which the arbitrator must choose between competing sets of proposals offered by labor and management for resolving the issues in contention (in essence, a "winner-take-all" format);
2. Final-offer (issue) arbitration: here the third party neutral selects the offer of either side on an issue-by-issue basis; and

3. Med-arb: the mediator becomes an arbitrator for those issues remaining unresolved after mediation.

What bothers analysts most about arbitration is that it imposes an externally derived solution upon parties who must live with it (and with each other) for the term of the agreement. Many believe that this strategy either (1) "chills" the parties toward a bargained compromise, because the arbitrator will split the difference between the positions, or (2) acts as a "narcotic," to the extent that each side perceives a more advantageous outcome to be gained by heading directly for impasse. The final-offer configurations were devised in response to these concerns. The belief was that incurring an arbitration "loss" (particularly significant given the incentive to make an extreme offer) would encourage greater effort at the table itself. Though results are mixed, the current research consensus appears to validate this claim for package selection, finds the opposite to be true for the discrete issue approach, and provides little or no support for the hypothesis that arbitration is habit forming (see Fossum, 1989, pp. 443–454, and Sylvia, 1989, pp. 124–145, for an extended discussion of this literature).

Strike Policy

The stance that subnational policymakers take toward strikes has significant implications for the importance of these impasse-resolution provisions. Should legislators outlaw any form of job action, the burden placed upon third party procedures is much heavier. Legislators must also be prepared to accept the political consequences of enforcement. Indeed, most states travel this route. The more militant antistrike jurisdictions of this number also enact a set of specific penalties to be applied in the event that the ban is violated. Such sanctions typically take two forms: penalties against individuals and/or penalties directed at the union. Strikers may be discharged, fined, demoted, or rehired on probation. The labor organization(s) involved may lose certification or automatic dues deduction. In contrast to these extremes, employees who join or refuse to cross a picket line are most often fined and are rarely terminated.[8]

The efficacy of such statutes continues to be debated. Reviewing the research, Veglahn (1983) finds little evidence to suggest that explicit sanctions work as effective deterrents to disruption; in fact, he concludes that "penalties may make the strike more difficult to settle, with negotiations being complicated by demands for amnesty or discussions of the use to which fine monies should be put" (p. 204).

An alternate view is that rather than being dysfunctional, strikes are instead a natural, healthy component of collective bargaining. Suggested in chapter 1, this perspective holds that where strikes are outlawed without exception, public employees armed with legal bargaining authority lack any real leverage because the employer has no tangible incentive to take their demands seriously. Some states have apparently considered and incorporated such thinking into policy. Rather than complete prohibition, a dozen or so permit what might best be labeled "managed" strikes. They grant their employees a qualified right to engage in work stoppages by establishing a series of procedural requirements designed to mitigate conflict. The limits they construct typically include one or more of the following provisions:

1. An essentiality distinction: only those employed in "nonessential" functions are allowed to strike;

2. Contract expiration/impasse-resolution limits: workers may walk out only after some minimum number of days has elapsed since the contract expired, and/or after all third party solutions have failed;

3. Notice of intent: many such laws require the employee representative to provide prior notice of the intent to strike (n days in advance); and

4. "Degree of Threat" provisos: all states with such policy reserve the right to ban any strike deemed to represent (approximating the most common language utilized) "a clear and present danger to public health, safety or welfare" (Rosenbloom, 1989, pp. 234–235).

Policymakers hope that by exhausting the tools of dispute resolution, providing a cooling-off period, and stopping short of a total ban, they can exercise greater control over the costs of disruption while allowing a measure of balance between the public interest and union power in the labor-management relationship.

Contract Administration

The final stage of the labor relations process is for the contract to be administered. The execution of negotiated terms is usually decentralized, so the details of this step are not regularly matters receiving formal legislative attention. Even so, two issues have significant impact upon the integrity of the process as a whole and therefore merit brief exposure.

In the first instance, it is important that a grievance system be hammered out. One real advantage of collective bargaining is that the need to interpret explicit contractual language forces the question of how to handle employee complaints. The communications stream thereby flows in two directions rather than one. This does necessitate, in the second case, the formulation of (1) an appeals process for disagreements unable to be resolved at the ''shop floor'' level and (2) a terminal step for the handful remaining viable once they have traversed such a hierarchy. Though specific routes may vary, the safest generalization is that most governments use some form of binding grievance arbitration to this end.

DESCRIPTIVE STATISTICS

With the broad set of policy issues faced by subnational policymakers now outlined, the final section of this chapter describes the nature of the decisions they have reached from grappling with the question of collective bargaining for their public employees over time. As suggested before, these data have been rather elusive until now. Fortunately, the database constructed by Valletta and Freeman (1985) at the National Bureau of Economic Research now provides a reasonably detailed view of that complex of statutory actions, opinions of state attorneys general, and judicial verdicts which constitute the subnational public sector labor relations environment. This dataset (diagrammed in table 3.1) covers fourteen measures of labor policy across the fifty states for thirty years (1955–1984), disaggregated by five occupations (i.e., state, police, fire, teachers, and other local employees). Tables 3.2 through 3.6 contain the relevant frequency distributions by policy provision across the states for each of these functions. The data are displayed in five-year increments for ease of presentation.

Three general observations most readily emerge from an initial glance across these five tables. First, a degree of diffusion is quite apparent in all cases, especially in the context of bargaining rights. The biggest move toward enactment falls around 1970. This is no real surprise for two reasons. If our previous propositions about the significance of Kennedy's action are correct, we would naturally expect to see a lag between EO 10988 and state activity. This jump may reflect the impact of the Supreme Court's subsequent decision in *Woodward* as well.

The second overall impression one gets from these tables is that the rate of policy change decreases by 1980. Here, too, there are at least two logical suspects. The fact that the final interval covered by the data is one year shorter is obvious. Yet it is also possible that the relative decline of the labor movement toward the end of the seventies

Table 3.1
Index of State Public Sector Bargaining Laws: Scaling Code

Bargaining Rights
0 = No Provision
1 = Prohibited
2 = Employer Authorized
3 = Proposals
4 = Meet and Confer
5 = Implied Duty
6 = Explicit Duty

Scope of Bargaining
0 = No Provision
1 = Excludes Compensation
2 = Includes Compensation

Representation & Election
0 = No Provision
1 = Non-exclusive
2 = Exclusive; No Procedure
3 = Exclusive; Procedure

Term of Recognition
0 = No Provision
1 = Post-Certification
2 = At Least 12 Mos.
3 = 12 Mos. and Expiration
4 = At Least 24 Mos.

Agency Shop
0 = No Provision
1 = Prohibited
2 = Negotiable
3 = Compulsory

Dues Checkoff
0 = No Provision
1 = Prohibited
2 = Negotiable
3 = Compulsory

Union Shop
0 = No Provision
1 = Prohibited
2 = Negotiable
3 = Compulsory

Right-to-Work
0 = No Law on Books
1 = Has Such a Law

Mediation: Availability
0 = No Provision
1 = Prohibited
2 = Voluntary
3 = Discretionary
4 = Mandatory

Fact-finding: Availability
0 = No Provision
1 = Prohibited
2 = Voluntary
3 = Discretionary
4 = Mandatory

Arbitration: Availability
0 = No Provision
1 = Prohibited
2 = Voluntary
3 = Discretionary
4 = Mandatory

Arbitration: Scope
0 = No Provision
1 = Non-Compensation Issues
2 = All Negotiable Issues

Arbitration: Type
0 = No Provision
1 = Conventional
2 = Final Offer-Issue
3 = Final Offer-Package
4 = Any Type May Be Used

Strike Policy
0 = No Provision
1 = Prohibited; Penalties
2 = Prohibited; No Penalties
3 = Permitted; Qualifications

Source: Adapted from Valletta and Freeman, 1985.

Table 3.2
Cross-State Policy Adoption, By Provision, Five-Year Intervals, 1955–1984: State Employees

Policy Provision	1955	1960	1965	1970	1975	1980	1984
A. Bargaining Rights							
No Provision	46	41	36	23	12	9	8
Prohibited	3	4	4	6	8	7	8
Employer Authorized	1	3	6	5	6	6	6
Proposals	0	2	3	1	1	1	1
Meet and Confer	0	0	1	4	3	4	3
Implied Duty	0	0	0	9	15	18	19
Explicit Duty	0	0	0	2	5	5	5
B. Scope of Bargaining							
No Provision	49	47	44	36	25	21	21
Excludes Compensation	0	0	0	1	1	1	1
Includes Compensation	1	3	6	13	24	28	28
C. Representation & Election							
No Provision	50	49	49	37	26	22	22
Non-exclusive	0	1	1	0	1	1	1
Exclusive; No Procedure	0	0	0	10	10	10	10
Exclusive; Procedure	0	0	0	3	13	17	17
D. Term of Recognition							
No Provision	50	50	50	43	32	29	29
Post-Certification	0	0	0	1	0	1	1
At Least 12 Mos.	0	0	0	5	7	7	7
12 Mos. and Expiration	0	0	0	0	10	12	12
At Least 24 Mos.	0	0	0	1	1	1	1
E. Agency Shop							
No Provision	43	42	40	40	27	22	20
Prohibited	7	8	10	10	15	15	15
Negotiable	0	0	0	0	6	9	11
Compulsory	0	0	0	0	2	4	4
F. Dues Checkoff							
No Provision	45	44	43	36	28	23	23
Prohibited	0	0	0	0	0	0	0
Negotiable	2	3	4	7	11	12	12
Compulsory	3	3	3	7	11	15	15
G. Union Shop							
No Provision	40	36	32	27	19	18	18
Prohibited	10	14	18	23	29	30	30
Negotiable	0	0	0	0	2	2	2
Compulsory	0	0	0	0	0	0	0

Table 3.2 (continued)

Policy Provision	1955	1960	1965	1970	1975	1980	1984
H. Right-to-Work							
No Law on Books	40	38	36	36	35	35	35
Has Such a Law	10	12	14	14	15	15	15
I. Mediation: Availability							
No Provision	48	48	47	39	30	26	26
Prohibited	0	0	0	0	0	0	0
Voluntary	0	0	0	1	0	0	0
Discretionary	2	2	3	10	16	18	18
Mandatory	0	0	0	0	4	6	6
J. Fact-finding: Availability							
No Provision	50	50	50	43	36	32	32
Prohibited	0	0	0	0	0	0	0
Voluntary	0	0	0	0	2	2	2
Discretionary	0	0	0	7	10	10	11
Mandatory	0	0	0	0	2	6	5
K. Arbitration: Availability							
No Provision	50	50	50	44	37	36	36
Prohibited	0	0	0	0	0	0	0
Voluntary	0	0	0	5	9	9	9
Discretionary	0	0	0	1	2	3	3
Mandatory	0	0	0	0	2	2	2
L. Arbitration: Scope							
No Provision	50	50	50	48	42	41	41
Non-Compensation Issues	0	0	0	1	3	3	3
All Negotiable Issues	0	0	0	1	5	6	6
M. Arbitration: Type							
No Provision	50	50	50	48	42	41	41
Conventional	0	0	0	2	6	6	6
Final Offer-Issue	0	0	0	0	0	1	1
Final Offer-Package	0	0	0	0	1	1	1
Any Type May Be Used	0	0	0	0	1	1	1
N. Strike Policy							
No Provision	42	39	35	26	16	12	11
Prohibited; Penalties	5	5	7	8	10	14	15
Prohibited; No Penalties	3	6	8	16	18	18	18
Permitted; Qualifications	0	0	0	0	6	6	6

Source: Calculated from Valletta and Freeman, 1985.

Table 3.3

Cross-State Policy Adoption, By Provision, Five-Year Intervals, 1955–1984: Police

Policy Provision	1955	1960	1965	1970	1975	1980	1984
A. Bargaining Rights							
No Provision	47	42	37	20	11	9	8
Prohibited	2	4	3	3	2	3	4
Employer Authorized	1	3	7	9	10	9	9
Proposals	0	1	2	1	1	1	1
Meet and Confer	0	0	1	2	1	1	1
Implied Duty	0	0	0	12	19	21	21
Explicit Duty	0	0	0	3	6	6	6
B. Scope of Bargaining							
No Provision	50	48	44	33	21	20	20
Excludes Compensation	0	0	0	0	0	0	0
Includes Compensation	0	2	6	17	29	30	30
C. Representation & Election							
No Provision	50	49	48	35	23	22	22
Non-exclusive	0	1	1	0	1	1	1
Exclusive; No Procedure	0	0	1	8	11	10	10
Exclusive; Procedure	0	0	0	7	15	17	17
D. Term of Recognition							
No Provision	50	50	49	40	27	26	26
Post-Certification	0	0	0	1	3	4	4
At Least 12 Mos.	0	0	1	5	11	10	10
12 Mos. and Expiration	0	0	0	4	9	10	10
At Least 24 Mos.	0	0	0	0	0	0	0
E. Agency Shop							
No Provision	43	42	40	38	28	23	22
Prohibited	7	8	10	10	13	16	15
Negotiable	0	0	0	2	8	10	12
Compulsory	0	0	0	0	1	1	1
F. Dues Checkoff							
No Provision	47	46	45	36	28	28	27
Prohibited	0	0	0	0	0	0	0
Negotiable	2	3	4	9	12	12	13
Compulsory	1	1	1	5	10	10	10
G. Union Shop							
No Provision	40	37	34	28	21	18	18
Prohibited	10	13	16	21	26	29	29
Negotiable	0	0	0	1	3	3	3
Compulsory	0	0	0	0	0	0	0

Table 3.3 (continued)

Policy Provision	1955	1960	1965	Year 1970	1975	1980	1984
H. Right-to-Work							
No Law on Books	40	38	36	36	35	35	35
Has Such a Law	10	12	14	14	15	15	15
I. Mediation: Availability							
No Provision	48	48	47	37	28	25	25
Prohibited	0	0	0	0	0	0	0
Voluntary	0	0	0	2	3	1	1
Discretionary	2	2	3	11	17	19	20
Mandatory	0	0	0	0	2	5	4
J. Fact-finding: Availability							
No Provision	50	50	48	40	33	32	32
Prohibited	0	0	0	0	0	0	0
Voluntary	0	0	0	1	1	1	1
Discretionary	0	0	1	8	13	11	12
Mandatory	0	0	1	1	3	6	5
K. Arbitration: Availability							
No Provision	50	50	50	40	30	29	29
Prohibited	0	0	0	0	0	0	0
Voluntary	0	0	0	5	9	6	7
Discretionary	0	0	0	4	6	8	8
Mandatory	0	0	0	1	5	7	6
L. Arbitration: Scope							
No Provision	50	50	50	44	35	31	32
Non-Compensation Issues	0	0	0	2	2	2	2
All Negotiable Issues	0	0	0	4	13	17	16
M. Arbitration: Type							
No Provision	50	50	50	45	35	31	32
Conventional	0	0	0	5	11	12	12
Final Offer-Issue	0	0	0	0	2	3	3
Final Offer-Package	0	0	0	0	1	1	1
Any Type May Be Used	0	0	0	0	1	3	2
N. Strike Policy							
No Provision	41	38	35	25	15	12	12
Prohibited; Penalties	6	6	7	9	13	17	17
Prohibited; No Penalties	3	6	8	16	21	20	20
Permitted; Qualifications	0	0	0	0	1	1	1

Source: Calculated from Valletta and Freeman, 1985.

Table 3.4
Cross-State Policy Adoption, By Provision, Five-Year Intervals, 1955–1984: Firefighters

Policy Provision	1955	1960	1965	1970	1975	1980	1984
A. Bargaining Rights							
No Provision	47	40	36	17	7	6	5
Prohibited	2	4	3	2	1	2	3
Employer Authorized	1	3	6	9	10	8	8
Proposals	0	1	2	2	2	2	2
Meet and Confer	0	1	1	3	3	3	3
Implied Duty	0	1	2	14	22	23	23
Explicit Duty	0	0	0	3	5	6	6
B. Scope of Bargaining							
No Provision	50	46	43	29	17	15	15
Excludes Compensation	0	0	0	0	0	0	0
Includes Compensation	0	4	7	21	33	35	35
C. Representation & Election							
No Provision	50	49	47	32	18	17	17
Non-exclusive	0	1	1	0	1	1	1
Exclusive; No Procedure	0	0	2	11	15	14	14
Exclusive; Procedure	0	0	0	7	16	18	18
D. Term of Recognition							
No Provision	50	50	49	39	26	24	24
Post-Certification	0	0	0	2	4	5	5
At Least 12 Mos.	0	0	1	5	10	10	10
12 Mos. and Expiration	0	0	0	4	10	11	11
At Least 24 Mos.	0	0	0	0	0	0	0
E. Agency Shop							
No Provision	43	42	40	38	27	22	21
Prohibited	7	8	10	10	13	16	15
Negotiable	0	0	0	2	9	11	13
Compulsory	0	0	0	0	1	1	1
F. Dues Checkoff							
No Provision	47	46	45	36	27	27	26
Prohibited	0	0	0	0	0	0	0
Negotiable	2	3	4	9	12	12	13
Compulsory	1	1	1	5	11	11	11
G. Union Shop							
No Provision	40	35	33	27	20	17	17
Prohibited	10	15	17	22	26	29	29
Negotiable	0	0	0	1	4	4	4
Compulsory	0	0	0	0	0	0	0

Table 3.4 (continued)

Policy Provision	1955	1960	1965	1970	1975	1980	1984
H. Right-to-Work							
No Law on Books	40	38	36	36	35	35	35
Has Such a Law	10	12	14	14	15	15	15
I. Mediation: Availability							
No Provision	48	48	47	37	27	24	24
Prohibited	0	0	0	0	0	0	0
Voluntary	0	0	0	2	3	1	1
Discretionary	2	2	3	11	18	20	20
Mandatory	0	0	0	0	2	5	5
J. Fact-finding: Availability							
No Provision	49	49	47	39	29	29	29
Prohibited	0	0	0	0	0	0	0
Voluntary	0	0	0	1	1	1	1
Discretionary	0	0	1	8	13	11	12
Mandatory	1	1	2	2	7	9	8
K. Arbitration: Availability							
No Provision	50	50	50	39	29	28	28
Prohibited	0	0	0	0	0	0	0
Voluntary	0	0	0	5	8	4	5
Discretionary	0	0	0	4	7	8	8
Mandatory	0	0	0	2	6	10	9
L. Arbitration: Scope							
No Provision	50	50	50	44	34	30	31
Non-Compensation Issues	0	0	0	2	2	2	2
All Negotiable Issues	0	0	0	4	14	18	17
M. Arbitration: Type							
No Provision	50	50	50	44	33	29	30
Conventional	0	0	0	6	13	12	12
Final Offer-Issue	0	0	0	0	2	3	3
Final Offer-Package	0	0	0	0	1	3	3
Any Type May Be Used	0	0	0	0	1	3	2
N. Strike Policy							
No Provision	41	37	33	22	11	10	10
Prohibited; Penalties	6	6	7	9	14	17	17
Prohibited; No Penalties	3	7	10	19	24	22	22
Permitted; Qualifications	0	0	0	0	1	1	1

Source: Calculated from Valletta and Freeman, 1985.

Table 3.5
Cross-State Policy Adoption, By Provision, Five-Year Intervals, 1955–1984:
Teachers

Policy Provision	Year						
	1955	1960	1965	1970	1975	1980	1984
A. Bargaining Rights							
No Provision	47	41	37	16	8	3	3
Prohibited	2	4	3	2	3	4	4
Employer Authorized	1	3	6	13	12	12	12
Proposals	0	1	2	1	1	1	1
Meet and Confer	0	0	1	3	1	0	0
Implied Duty	0	1	1	14	21	25	24
Explicit Duty	0	0	0	1	4	5	6
B. Scope of Bargaining							
No Provision	50	47	44	30	24	20	20
Excludes Compensation	0	0	0	0	0	0	0
Includes Compensation	0	3	6	20	26	30	30
C. Representation & Election							
No Provision	50	49	48	32	22	18	18
Non-exclusive	0	1	1	1	2	1	1
Exclusive; No Procedure	0	0	1	8	9	8	8
Exclusive; Procedure	0	0	0	9	17	23	23
D. Term of Recognition							
No Provision	50	50	50	38	29	22	22
Post-Certification	0	0	0	1	2	4	4
At Least 12 Mos.	0	0	0	6	8	10	10
12 Mos. and Expiration	0	0	0	3	8	10	11
At Least 24 Mos.	0	0	0	2	3	4	3
E. Agency Shop							
No Provision	43	42	40	37	28	20	19
Prohibited	7	8	10	12	15	17	16
Negotiable	0	0	0	1	6	11	13
Compulsory	0	0	0	0	1	2	2
F. Dues Checkoff							
No Provision	47	46	45	38	30	23	23
Prohibited	0	0	0	0	0	0	0
Negotiable	2	3	4	7	10	13	13
Compulsory	1	1	1	5	10	14	14
G. Union Shop							
No Provision	40	36	33	26	17	13	13
Prohibited	10	14	17	24	31	37	37
Negotiable	0	0	0	0	2	0	0
Compulsory	0	0	0	0	0	0	0

Table 3.5 (continued)

Policy Provision	1955	1960	1965	1970	1975	1980	1984
H. Right-to-Work							
No Law on Books	40	38	36	36	35	35	35
Has Such a Law	10	12	14	14	15	15	15
I. Mediation: Availability							
No Provision	48	48	47	37	27	20	20
Prohibited	0	0	0	0	0	0	0
Voluntary	0	0	0	3	5	3	3
Discretionary	2	2	3	9	15	20	21
Mandatory	0	0	0	1	3	7	6
J. Fact-finding: Availability							
No Provision	50	50	49	38	31	23	23
Prohibited	0	0	0	0	0	0	0
Voluntary	0	0	0	2	2	2	1
Discretionary	0	0	1	8	14	18	20
Mandatory	0	0	0	2	3	7	6
K. Arbitration: Availability							
No Provision	50	50	50	43	36	32	33
Prohibited	0	0	0	1	1	1	0
Voluntary	0	0	0	3	10	11	11
Discretionary	0	0	0	3	3	5	5
Mandatory	0	0	0	0	0	1	1
L. Arbitration: Scope							
No Provision	50	50	50	47	44	40	40
Non-Compensation Issues	0	0	0	2	2	2	2
All Negotiable Issues	0	0	0	1	4	8	8
M. Arbitration: Type							
No Provision	50	50	50	47	44	40	40
Conventional	0	0	0	3	5	6	6
Final Offer-Issue	0	0	0	0	0	2	2
Final Offer-Package	0	0	0	0	0	1	1
Any Type May Be Used	0	0	0	0	1	1	1
N. Strike Policy							
No Provision	41	38	35	23	13	9	9
Prohibited; Penalties	6	6	7	10	13	18	18
Prohibited; No Penalties	3	6	8	16	18	15	15
Permitted; Qualifications	0	0	0	1	6	8	8

Source: Calculated from Valletta and Freeman, 1985.

Table 3.6
Cross-State Policy Adoption, By Provision, Five-Year Intervals, 1955–1984: Other Local Employees

Policy Provision	1955	1960	1965	1970	1975	1980	1984
A. Bargaining Rights							
No Provision	47	41	37	19	12	10	9
Prohibited	2	4	3	3	3	4	5
Employer Authorized	1	3	6	9	11	9	9
Proposals	0	1	2	1	1	1	1
Meet and Confer	0	0	1	3	2	2	2
Implied Duty	0	1	1	13	16	18	18
Explicit Duty	0	0	0	2	5	6	6
B. Scope of Bargaining							
No Provision	50	47	44	32	24	22	22
Excludes Compensation	0	0	0	0	0	0	0
Includes Compensation	0	3	6	18	26	28	28
C. Representation & Election							
No Provision	50	49	48	34	25	23	23
Non-exclusive	0	1	1	0	1	1	1
Exclusive; No Procedure	0	0	1	9	9	9	9
Exclusive; Procedure	0	0	0	7	15	17	17
D. Term of Recognition							
No Provision	50	50	50	40	29	27	27
Post-Certification	0	0	0	1	2	3	3
At Least 12 Mos.	0	0	0	5	9	9	9
12 Mos. and Expiration	0	0	0	4	10	11	11
At Least 24 Mos.	0	0	0	0	0	0	0
E. Agency Shop							
No Provision	43	42	40	38	28	24	23
Prohibited	7	8	10	10	13	15	14
Negotiable	0	0	0	2	8	10	12
Compulsory	0	0	0	0	1	1	1
F. Dues Checkoff							
No Provision	47	46	45	37	29	28	27
Prohibited	0	0	0	0	0	0	0
Negotiable	2	3	4	8	12	12	13
Compulsory	1	1	1	5	9	10	10
G. Union Shop							
No Provision	40	36	33	28	21	19	19
Prohibited	10	14	17	21	26	28	28
Negotiable	0	0	0	1	3	3	3
Compulsory	0	0	0	0	0	0	0

Table 3.6 (continued)

Policy Provision	1955	1960	1965	1970	1975	1980	1984
H. Right-to-Work							
No Law on Books	40	38	36	36	35	35	35
Has Such a Law	10	12	14	14	15	15	15
I. Mediation: Availability							
No Provision	48	48	47	36	28	25	25
Prohibited	0	0	0	0	0	0	0
Voluntary	0	0	0	2	2	0	1
Discretionary	2	2	3	12	17	18	18
Mandatory	0	0	0	0	3	7	6
J. Fact-finding: Availability							
No Provision	50	50	49	40	35	32	32
Prohibited	0	0	0	0	0	0	0
Voluntary	0	0	0	1	1	1	1
Discretionary	0	0	1	8	12	10	11
Mandatory	0	0	0	1	2	7	6
K. Arbitration: Availability							
No Provision	50	50	50	42	35	33	33
Prohibited	0	0	0	0	0	0	0
Voluntary	0	0	0	5	12	11	11
Discretionary	0	0	0	3	3	5	5
Mandatory	0	0	0	0	0	1	1
L. Arbitration: Scope							
No Provision	50	50	50	46	42	39	39
Non-Compensation Issues	0	0	0	3	3	3	3
All Negotiable Issues	0	0	0	1	5	8	8
M. Arbitration: Type							
No Provision	50	50	50	46	42	39	39
Conventional	0	0	0	4	7	7	7
Final Offer-Issue	0	0	0	0	0	2	2
Final Offer-Package	0	0	0	0	0	1	1
Any Type May Be Used	0	0	0	0	1	1	1
N. Strike Policy							
No Provision	41	38	35	23	15	13	13
Prohibited; Penalties	6	6	7	8	9	12	12
Prohibited; No Penalties	3	6	8	18	19	17	17
Permitted; Qualifications	0	0	0	1	7	8	8

Source: Calculated from Valletta and Freeman, 1985.

suggested by so many analysts has some responsibility for this apparent trend.

The third thing that stands out are those categories of potential policy action not utilized by decision makers across the time points in the period represented here. No state prohibits dues checkoff, mediation, or fact-finding. Only Maryland outlaws arbitration, and it does so only for teachers between 1970 and 1980. With the exception of this outlier, it is equally consistent with our earlier logic that no jurisdiction finds a rationale to make union shop compulsory.

With this overview in mind, we now turn to an analysis of these data on a provision-by-provision basis. The results of this effort are even more interesting, particularly to the extent that they vary across occupations and over time. The conclusions drawn from this exercise constitute the balance of this chapter.

Bargaining Rights

Over the course of the period there is a decided move toward bargaining across the states. A duty implied somewhere in the law which requires the employer to engage in negotiations with its employees is far and away the most frequent category of rights beginning in 1975. When the jurisdictions making this obligation explicit are included, mandated negotiation becomes the majority outcome across all governments. Policy covering state employees is the only exception to this generalization, probably because of the fact that nearly twice as many states explicitly prohibit bargaining for this group. Only a handful or fewer in the other four cases take such a stance.

The Scope of Bargaining

These data suggest a finding of similar shape here. More than half (in the case of firefighters, many more) of all jurisdictions make compensation a negotiable subject by 1975. Once again it is policy covering state workers which provides the singular violation of this rule (in 1975). In fact, only Wisconsin (1970) and New Mexico (1975, 1980, and 1984) specifically exclude the money issue at any time point.[9]

Representation and Election

Among those adopting policy dealing with the mechanics of representation, all but one state in each instance provide exclusive recognition to the majority labor organization. A significant number do so without establishing a set of specific certification procedures, but the bias clearly favors explicit mechanisms. Across occupations, it is Arizona (1975, 1980, and 1984), Minnesota (1960 and 1965), and California (teachers, 1970 and 1975) which are the exceptions. (Though not shown here, Iowa takes the same position across all functions from 1971 through 1974.)

Term of Recognition

The states most frequently neglect this issue when deliberating labor policy. "No provision" is the majority outcome for all cases but firefighters and teachers in 1980 and 1984. Those adopting some stance favor a twelve-month term (from or regardless of contract expiration). Indeed, only the latter group, in less than a handful of jurisdictions between 1970 and 1984, receives the security of two-year certification. This is also true for state employees in New Hampshire (1970 and 1975) and Michigan (1980 and 1984).

Agency Shop

A majority of governments in each case address this question by 1980, though like the term of recognition, the most common outcome is policy silence. Next in line is explicit prohibition, no real surprise considering that the Right-to-Work states observed here typically outlaw this form of security and union shop as well. The remainder (about one-quarter of the total) makes this a negotiable item, and a very small number choose the compulsory route.

Dues Checkoff

Congruent with the logic of our earlier discussion, the jurisdictions represented here have less difficulty with this weakest form of union security. More than half apparently find no reason to address this concern explicitly, except for state employees and teachers in 1980 and 1984. Among adopters the split is fairly even between those making automatic deduction a permissible bargaining subject and their counterparts, who define it as a compulsory management obligation.

Union Shop

The data here also appear to confirm our expectations about this strongest form of union security. They suggest a widespread, antagonistic response to the issue of compulsory union membership. At maximum, only a small handful make such provisions negotiable at any time point.

Right-to-Work

The incidence of these laws increased 50 percent between 1955 and 1984. Most of this change occurred by 1965. Though not shown here, five additional states now have similar language somewhere on the books (making this a thirty-to-twenty split at present).

We now turn to provisions targeted at the disruption component of collective bargaining—those associated with impasse-resolution strategies and with strikes.

Mediation

Of the three options, these data suggest that subnational legislators find this third-party procedure most appealing. Those speaking to the matter choose also to make it easily accessible. In most cases the PERB or PERC may initiate mediation either unilaterally or upon the request of either party. The fact that only a limited number mandates a mediator implies two additional hypotheses: (1) that they wish to retain control over impasses administratively, and/or (2) that they hope to resolve any disputes that arise without outside intervention if possible.

Fact-Finding

State-level policymakers appear to be less interested in this technique. Only in the case of teachers (in 1980 and 1984) do a majority of governments adopt any statement. As with mediation, it is the discretionary route they prefer.

Arbitration

These provisions receive even less attention. Arbitration is apparently deliberated most often in the contexts of police and fire protection, and there exists less consensus across the states about the most desirable form of its initiation. It is most frequently true that both parties to an impasse involving state, teaching, and other local employees must consent for arbitration to occur. Yet for uniformed personnel this step is about as readily implemented on a discretionary or mandatory basis. This makes intuitive sense given traditional worries about the potential costs of strikes in these spheres.

An even smaller number (about 20 percent) spend time thinking any further about mechanics. Once again decision makers are most likely to flesh out the details for police and firefighters. The majority view on scope supports the inclusion of all negotiable issues, as it does the use of arbitration in its conventional form across occupations. Few jurisdictions seem willing to experiment with alternative configurations.

Strike Policy

The official line toward strikes is about as predictable. There are only two mild surprises in evidence. The first is that so many governments (approximately one-quarter) take no position. The second is that it is Montana which grants its police a limited strike beginning in 1975. This is also true for its firefighters in that year; it is neighboring Idaho which permits the same for this latter group in 1980 and 1984. Otherwise, we could certainly anticipate the two-thirds which ban strikes (with or without specific sanctions) as well as the general definition of essential service apparently at work across jurisdictions.

Summary

Though there is plenty of variation to be explained between and within states over time, it is the degree of cross-occupational similarity which is arguably most striking (no pun intended) in these tables. Speaking across functions, the modal state adopts no policy until sometime after 1970. At that time it is most likely to establish (1) an implied duty to bargain (2) on a range of issues which includes compensation; it will: (3) outlaw union shop and (4) prohibit strikes (without explicit penalties).

There are only a few exceptions to this generalization. Scope determinations for state employees do not emerge in a majority until 1975. Firefighters and teachers appear strong enough to win exclusive recognition during the same period. In 1980 and 1984, teachers are most likely to face specific legal sanctions in response to any job actions in which they might participate. Overall, subnational public sector labor policy remains fairly underdeveloped since its origins in the middle 1950s. Something less than a majority has constructed comprehensive frameworks for collective bargaining.

If "what governments do" is less than we might expect, questions about "why they do it" and "what difference it makes" remain open, if not even more intriguing, in regard to the subset which does take action in this area. Chapter 4 attempts to provide an answer to the first question and chapter 5 grapples with the second.

NOTES

1. Hindsight tells us that this was a Pyrrhic victory for the public sector side of the labor movement. For although Lloyd-LaFollette did allow federal workers to petition Congress either individually or jointly, the Act restricted these guarantees to members of unions that did not authorize the use of the strike. Strikes by federal employees remain illegal and enforced (e.g., Reagan and PATCO). Lloyd-LaFollette also supports two of our classic conceptual propositions about agenda-building; the strategic location of postal workers was quite important to their access to Congress, and the remarkable longevity of the limits imposed by the Act are a good example of the importance of past policy to the shape of subsequent agendas (e.g., Cobb and Elder, 1983).

2. In fact, two bills introduced to the House in 1989 by Representative William Clay (D-MO) attempted to guarantee the right of law enforcement personnel and firefighters to organize and to bargain collectively, to establish impasse procedures, and to specify unfair labor practices for both the employer and employee organizations. Like existing federal law, the proposed legislation would have prohibited strikes or work slowdowns (IPMA, 1989, p. 8). Though these measures did not survive the session, similar initiatives make a regular appearance across congressional calendars.

3. As indicated in the opinion, the FLSA contained an exemption for "executive, administrative or professional personnel"; the 1974 Amendments supplemented this list with "those individuals holding public elective office or serving such an officeholder in one of several specific capacities." In the subsequent furor over the decision, few appear to note the potential size of the exempted class or the superficial irony of the exemptions in general.

4. In the discussion that follows, there can always be, of course, an additional policy outcome: no provision. Though the number of states refusing to take up the issue of collective bargaining began to decline rapidly not long after the promulgation of EO 10988, there remains a handful with no law of any sort on the books. The relevant descriptive statistics on these trends are presented in the concluding section of this chapter.

5. There is a number of notable exceptions to these generalizations. Nevada, for example, is one of the few states to make pay a mandatory bargaining issue. California and Connecticut are also quite progressive where scope is concerned. The former excludes very few personnel matters from the process, and the latter bars only recruitment and promotion activities of its civil service commissions from discussion (Gordon, 1986, p. 369; Bent and Reeves, 1978, p. 61). As Gordon suggests, the states exhibit "predictable variety."

6. One caveat is necessary before we proceed with this discussion. The description of the process thus far may make it appear that bargaining is established through a series of neat and successive steps. Though systematic analysis requires such order, the politics of the question make this, in many cases, a messy business. We have already made the point, for example, that scope is usually defined incrementally over time. Most significant to the immediate issue is the fact that (consistent with *Woodward*) organizing activity by public employees can certainly precede any legal authorization for bargaining (in any of its forms). Yet as we will see in chapter 5, unionization in an environment of policy silence or hostility is very difficult to sustain, probably because success (achieving both threshold membership and the right to bargain) is so much more uncertain. The odds against such policy-forcing activity are quite imposing.

7. To be accurate, this last component of the description (i.e., unwanted service) did not emerge until agency shop was tested in the courts. In *D. Louis Abood et al. v. Detroit Board of Education*, the Supreme Court upheld the validity of these provisions in the public sector and constructed such a rebate (Holley and Jennings, 1980, p. 335). We should add one other note. Some states also consider or enact the "maintenance of membership" form of union security. Where present, employees joining the union must remain members for the duration of the contract. We omit this discussion from the text only because the issue involved is less substantive than procedural.

8. The most common outcome is for the individual to lose his or her wages for the duration of an illegal strike. New York's Taylor law is a much-cited exception to this rule. Public employees in this state lose two days' pay for each day out on strike.

9. There is an operationalization issue particularly observable here as well. As suggested earlier in the chapter, scope determinations can be quite detailed given the sovereignty issue involved and therefore the usual penchant for some form of "management rights" language in the law. Because Valletta and Freeman provide no explicit indication on the topic, one can only guess that they chose this functional form for the indicator (1) as the strongest response they could muster to measure some intractable conceptual complexity, (2) because of the relevance of the compensation issue at the federal level, and/or (3) given the implications that excluding wages might have for union power in general.

4 Why They Do It: Antecedents of Public Sector Labor Policy

If we now have a better idea of what governments do, this chapter addresses the second task of policy analysis framed by Dye—why they do it. In this chapter policy is the dependent variable. The intent is to explore some of the reasons for which subnational policymakers decide to adopt or decide to refrain from adopting a system of collective bargaining, defined in various fashions, for their public employees.

It may certainly be argued that the causes of public policy are less important or interesting than the consequences of such actions. Yet if the intent of this research is to provide a wider perspective on policy activity in this sphere, then this piece of the larger puzzle must be set in place. In this sense (and consistent with the plan elaborated in chapter 2) policy plays an intervening role between exogenous circumstances and endogenous outcomes.

THE LITERATURE

It was also suggested in chapter 2 that previous research on this question is quite slim. An extensive literature search unearthed a mere two studies which examine policy determination in the public sector labor relations context. Only Kochan (1973) and Faber and Martin (1979) offer any specific guidance here.

Kochan employs the systems paradigm to approach this task (as described in the second chapter). He constructs an ordinal index of state public sector bargaining laws covering five employee groups (police, firefighters, teachers, local, and state employees) as of 1972. He then performs a stepwise regression of this index upon a host of potential (socioeconomic and political) explanatory indicators, a list derived primarily from the work of the early cross-state comparative policy analysts in political science (e.g., Dawson and Robinson, 1963; Dye, 1966; Hofferbert, 1968; Sharkansky and Hofferbert, 1969). Kochan finds that change in income per capita (1960–1970), state per capita expenditures of government, and innovativeness (i.e., Walker's (1971) innovation index) jointly explain about one-third of the policy variance.

Faber and Martin (1979) examine the relationship between urbanization, ideology, and the early enactment of state collective bargaining legislation for teachers.[1] They correlate a dichotomous measure of enactment at two time points (1968 and 1975), first, with interval and dichotomous indicators of urbanization and, second, with a "conservatism index" of the voting record for each state's congressional delegation. They find that both urbanization and ideology (i.e., conservatism, to be elaborated momentarily) correlate with enactment: states with urban populations have enacted policy covering teachers by 1968 (the 1975 correlations are negligible), and conservative states are less likely than their more liberal counterparts to adopt collective bargaining legislation. Note that the latter correlations between policy and conservatism are consistently stronger than those between the policy variable and urbanization, and they are strongest for the 1975 measure of policy and when meet-and-confer states are excluded from the analysis.

Taken together, the findings of these two analyses tell us that subnational public sector labor policy (specifically, 1972 policy in the former and teacher collective bargaining provisions in the latter) is the result of per capita income and expenditures, urbanization, innovativeness, and ideology. These findings are intuitively appealing. Conventional wisdom (or fear) holds that unionization means vastly increased labor costs for the employer. We have already observed that research on the wage effects of unionization indicates only marginal increases which vary across occupations (i.e., Freeman, 1986; Methe and Perry, 1980); yet it may be the case that, acting on this conventional perception, only those jurisdictions which can "afford" collective bargaining provide it to part or all of their public workforce.

It also makes sense to suggest that the relationship between urbanization and policy has two dimensions, one related to the necessity of providing services and the other a function of political culture. Sheer demand for schools, police, and fire protection obviously expands with the size of the urban population. In addition, a larger pool of public employees enhances the significance of the personnel function and increases the susceptibility of the workforce to organizing efforts as well. The outcome of this logic is that policy is enacted in response to unionization, in line with the contention discussed above.

In the second case, policy designed to facilitate the labor relations process may be the result of a more "enlightened" urban population. "Conventional wisdom," according to Faber and Martin, "holds that collective bargaining in the public sector is more acceptable to urban and/ or liberal populations than it is to populations that are more rural and/or conservative" (1979, p. 151). States containing more "liberal" urban populations may wish to provide (and to provide earlier than other jurisdictions) their public employees with an environment reflecting the traditional claims for collective bargaining in the private sector (i.e., the Wellington and Winter logic described in chapter 1): legal frameworks which recognize the need for labor peace, workplace democracy, pluralism, and the counterweight to employer power provided by collective employee action.

FURTHER TESTING

It remains to be seen whether the findings drawn from this (small) literature apply across other occupations and at different time points. The analysis to follow attempts to address this issue. The goal, of course, is to develop a more complete explanation of the variance in this patchwork of subnational public sector labor policies extant within and across the states.

Policy and Ideology

The relationship between policy and ideology is particularly intriguing. Although policy may be sometimes (or often) the negative or reactive product of actual or anticipated labor disruption, it may be in other times or locations tangible evidence of a more positive cultural attitude toward the right of public employees to organize and to pursue their interests regardless of employer. The tension between employee rights and public prerogative is not readily diminished.

While data on specific attitudes toward public sector bargaining required to resolve this question are unavailable, the general "liberalism" finding of Faber and Martin can be tested with greater rigor. There are at least two reasons for skepticism about their conclusion. First, it is derived from policy covering teachers only, limited to two temporal snapshots. The definition of what constitutes an "essential service" occupation may be unclear, but it usually revolves around the political costs associated with service disruption. A definitive clarification of whether a teachers' strike is uniformly more severe than one of sanitation employees or a bout of "blue flu" cannot be provided. It does seem logical, however, to argue that fear of strikes or "job actions" by these segments of the public workforce will result in a statutory attempt to preempt them (or to structure the bargaining process in general). Whether similar policy provisions will be applied to other categories of state or local employees, for reasons of ideology or risk aversion, remains in question.

The second problem lies in the policy indicator Faber and Martin employ, a dichotomous measure of adoption. As described and utilized in chapter 3, data regarding "what governments do" have improved substantially since their writing. The Valletta and Freeman data mean that a more complete picture of policy is available for use here as well.

In an attempt to reassess the relationship between ideology and policy on a broader scale, the NBER data set is adopted as the relevant policy measure. For state ideology an expanded version of the index used by Faber and Martin is employed. They construct a "conservatism" index based upon the voting records of each state's congressional delegation, a common proxy for this concept. Scores on the index represent the mean difference between the annual "scorecards" produced by two polar opposites on the political spectrum (i.e., Americans for Constitutional Action, Americans for Democratic Action). Faber and Martin subtract the ADA from the ACA score for each state's congressional delegation (representatives and senators) and then average these numbers across three rating periods (1972, 1974, and 1976). Going back to the original data (*Congressional Quarterly*, 1960–1985), the same operation was performed to get annual figures running from 1960 through 1984.[2] As in the original construction, the higher (lower) the score, the more conservative (liberal) the state.[3]

For explanatory purposes, a mean score was computed for each state across the entire period of observation (1960–1984). The results of this procedure appear in table 4.1. The fact that nineteen of the twenty (current) Right-to-Work states fall on the conservative end of the continuum adds face validation to the consensual validity associated with this proxy. Only Iowa scores in the lower half of the rankings. Further examination of the data reveals that Iowa's scores essentially flip in 1973. Its moderately conservative mean of 24.0 from 1960–72 changes sign to a liberal score of −21.9 during the 1973–84 period. Even so, Iowa's 1955 Right-to-Work statute remains on the books.

Table 4.1
Mean Score on the Conservatism Index, By State, 1960–1984

Rank	State	Mean Score	Rank	State	Mean Score
1	*Virginia	67.6	26	Kentucky	5.1
2	*Missisippi	66.8	27	Indiana	4.4
3	*Nebraska	64.7	28	*Iowa	0.0
4	*South Carolina	49.5	29	Illinois	0.0
5	*Kansas	47.7	30	Colorado	- 1.8
6	*North Carolina	46.7	31	Alaska	- 5.3
7	*Alabama	45.6	32	Missouri	- 9.0
8	*Georgia	43.5	33	Pennsylvania	-11.1
9	Idaho	40.1	34	California	-12.5
10	*Arizona	39.8	35	Michigan	-15.9
11	*Louisiana	35.6	36	Wisconsin	-16.5
12	*Utah	34.2	37	Minnesota	-19.5
13	*Florida	31.5	38	Vermont	-20.3
14	*Wyoming	31.2	39	West Virginia	-24.8
15	*Nevada	28.5	40	New York	-26.8
16	*Texas	25.9	41	Maryland	-27.6
17	New Hampshire	23.2	42	Oregon	-27.8
18	Oklahoma	22.2	43	Montana	-32.4
19	*Tennessee	21.9	44	Maine	-32.8
20	New Mexico	18.0	45	Washington	-33.1
21	*Arkansas	17.8	46	New Jersey	-39.3
22	Ohio	16.6	47	Connecticut	-48.4
23	Delaware	15.2	48	Hawaii	-51.0
24	*North Dakota	12.5	49	Massachusetts	-55.2
25	*South Dakota	10.2	50	Rhode Island	-66.0

Source: Calculated from Valletta and Freman, 1985.

In the context of the policy data (i.e., table 3.1) the modal Right-to-Work state explicitly prohibits bargaining, agency, and union shop provisions, as well as strikes. It is no surprise, of course, that the more conservative southern and western states make up the bulk of those jurisdictions adopting such an antibargaining stance. What is more interesting is the relationship between "conservatism" and policy over time.

In order to examine this relationship, it was at first decided that an additive index should be constructed across the policy measures in table 3.1, a simple sum across all 14 categories. For example, a state with no provision in any category would receive a score of 0, and a state with policy reflecting the highest ordinal values for each dimension of policy could achieve a score of 46 (an unlikely occurrence, unless it had an unenforced Right-to-Work law remaining on the books despite subsequent enactments to the contrary). Policy scores were computed in this manner for each occupation at all 24 time points, and scores were also added across the five functions to obtain a grand (i.e., cross-occupation) measure of any state's stance toward collective bargaining.

The relevant assumption at work here was that the higher the additive policy score, the more "liberal" the attitude toward bargaining. An examination of table 3.1 supports this contention with one exception. A state having no explicit policy at time t which subsequently adopts prohibitions of one sort or another at $t+1$ is moving in the opposite direction.

To correct this complication in the Valletta and Freeman scale (and given the uses to which it will be put below), each policy prohibition in table 3.1 was reassigned a value of -1 and its counterpart codes adjusted accordingly. The indicator for "Collective Bargaining Rights," for example, was reconfigured to run from "Collective bargaining prohibited" (-1) to "Duty to bargain explicit" ($+5$). The measures for agency shop, dues checkoff, and union shop were reformulated as -1 ("Prohibited") to $+2$ ("Compulsory") and so on. Besides these four, the Right-to-Work law, mediation, fact-finding, arbitration, and strike policy variables were similarly re-scaled. (Note that the Right-to-Work codes became -1 (law) and 0 (no law), and that the strike policy continuum assumed a -2 ("Prohibited with penalties specified") to $+1$ ("Permitted") structure). Scores on the revised additive index for each occupation therefore have a potential range of -10 to $+36$. The details of sensitivity analysis performed to gauge the significance of this new scaling scheme to the results obtained below support this decision, and are discussed in appendix 5.1. Table 4.2 provides a look at the cross-occupation scores on this index, by state, in five-year increments for the 1960–1984 period (range $= -50$ to $+180$).

A second critical assumption is alluded to above and should be made explicit as well. These measures of policy are inexact reflections of the "true" bargaining environment in any state to the extent that local jurisdictions adopt bargaining mechanisms which differ from state policy. Missouri, for example, provides meet-and-confer rights to public employees, but the City of Columbia bargains with its workforce anyway. The tradeoff between internal and external validity is very real in this situation. The analysis to follow is based upon the observable contention that state policy is the single most important determinant of the bargaining environment facing public employees within its confines.

These concerns aside, figure 4.1 charts the simple correlations between the conservatism index and the state labor policy scores in

Table 4.2
Cross-Occupation Scores on the Policy Index, By State, Five-Year Increments, 1960–1984

State	1960	1965	1970	1975	1980	1984
Alabama	-25	-25	-20	-18	-18	-18
Alaska	15	15	15	97	105	105
Arizona	-15	-15	-15	5	7	7
Arkansas	-20	-20	-15	-14	-14	-14
California	3	17	27	44	54	63
Colorado	0	0	0	0	-4	-4
Connecticut	0	0	59	59	117	117
Delaware	0	1	85	85	84	86
Florida	-15	-15	-15	-6	80	80
Georgia	0	-2	-1	5	5	5
Hawaii	0	0	0	116	119	119
Idaho	4	4	4	23	25	25
Illinois	6	11	10	14	9	9
Indiana	0	0	5	22	19	21
Iowa	-10	-10	-10	25	95	95
Kansas	-10	-10	-10	56	60	60
Kentucky	0	0	0	21	21	21
Louisiana	0	0	5	10	9	9
Maine	0	0	72	90	83	83
Maryland	0	0	12	12	12	12
Massachusetts	30	28	71	94	98	82
Michigan	2	2	56	69	81	82
Minnesota	-10	-10	19	112	112	112
Mississippi	0	-15	-15	-15	-15	-15
Missouri	0	0	18	18	18	18
Montana	0	0	0	88	103	103
Nebraska	-20	-20	46	70	67	67
Nevada	0	0	47	43	57	54
New Hampshire	0	0	10	24	75	75
New Jersey	0	0	55	55	77	82
New Mexico	0	0	4	16	16	16
New York	-10	-10	60	64	74	74
North Carolina	-5	-5	-5	-5	-5	-5
North Dakota	-10	-10	1	1	3	3
Ohio	-5	-5	-5	-15	-12	-12
Oklahoma	0	0	0	28	29	29
Oregon	0	20	60	125	115	115
Pennsylvania	-10	-10	18	79	79	79

Table 4.2 (continued)

State	1960	1965	1970	1975	1980	1984
Rhode Island	3	27	69	82	84	84
South Carolina	-10	-10	-10	-15	-10	-10
South Dakota	-10	-10	25	57	55	50
Tennessee	0	0	0	0	12	6
Texas	-25	-25	-19	11	11	11
Utah	-15	-15	-5	-5	-5	-5
Vermont	0	0	80	98	98	98
Virginia	-5	3	3	-22	-30	-30
Washington	0	0	65	97	96	96
West Virginia	2	17	17	17	17	17
Wisconsin	15	26	37	80	94	94
Wyoming	0	-15	-2	-2	-2	-2

Source: Calculated from Valletta and Freeman, 1985.

successive cross sections over the course of the period. The moderate negative relationship (approximately -0.40 across all groups) which exists between these variables in 1960 decreases somewhat and then rapidly strengthens in magnitude beginning in about 1970. While most strongly negative during the next ten years (approximately -0.65), the level of correlation moderates to about -0.45 by 1984. Also notable is the relative consistency of the correlations across occupations during the period. The difference in coefficients never exceeds 0.20 (i.e., in 1967 and 1984), further substantiating the policy similarities observed in chapter 3.

In sum, figure 4.1 provides a reasonably clear signal that the relationship between ideology and policy is strong and inverse, supporting the conventional hypothesis. Read in the context of table 4.2, it becomes apparent that the early adopters acted to prohibit bargaining in various ways (typically the conservative states). Most continue this coverage or provide only weak authorization for their employees throughout the period. Their more liberal counterparts, on the other hand, begin to establish legal frameworks which facilitate public sector bargaining by about 1970. During the decade to follow, the essentially bimodal spread toward the policy extremes of prohibition and mandated negotiation more closely reflects the distribution of scores on the conservative index, moderating somewhat by 1984.

Figure 4.1
Conservatism and State Labor Policy, Correlations: 1960, 1962, 1964–1984

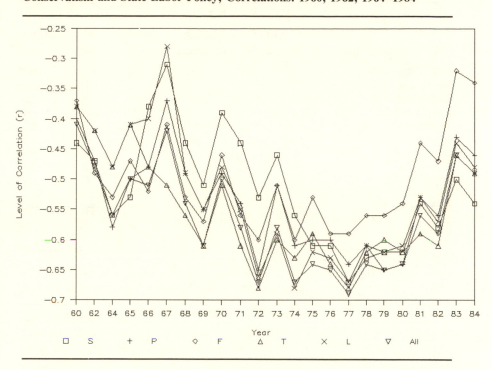

Ideology in the Context of Other Determinants

The next analytical task is to determine whether the relationship between conservatism and policy holds up in the context of the alternative
antecedents derived from the literature: urbanization, per capita income
and expenditures, innovation, and unionization.[4] Table 4.3 contains the
intercorrelations between these potential explanatory variables (indicators
to be used in regression analyses, momentarily). Table 4.4 provides the
correlations between each of these hypothesized antecedents and the six
policy measures.

The strongest (negative) correlation in table 4.3 exists between conservatism and the percent of the public workforce that is unionized. While
there is, of course, no way to attribute causation from a correlation, this
figure provides at least sketchy support for the earlier contention that
unionism prospers in a sympathetic (in this case, ideological) environment. That early organizing by public employees instead drives ideology
seems less likely if it can be assumed that the proxy employed for the
latter accesses some portion of the variance associated with a more durable

Table 4.3
Intercorrelations Between Explanatory Variables, 1972–1984

	INPC	URBAN	ACADA	INNOV	UNION <a>
EXPC <b>	.63	.00	.00	.38	.26
INPC <c>		.25	-.10	.49	.23
URBAN <d>			-.20	.16	.50
ACADA <e>				-.25	-.65
INNOV <f>					.38

Data, sources, and notes:
   (a) Percent public sector organized, by state, 1972, 1973–1980, 1982. U.S. Department of Commerce, Bureau of the Census, *Labor Management Relations in State and Local Government*, 1972–1980; Troy and Sheflin, 1985.
   (b) Total per capita general expenditures, by state, 1972–1984. U.S. Department of Commerce, Bureau of the Census, *Statistical Abstract of the United States*, 1974–1981, 1984–1987.
   (c) Personal income per capita, by state, 1972–1984. *Ibid.*, 1973–1980, 1985–1987.
   (d) Percent urban, by state, 1970, 1980. *Ibid.*, 1987.
   (e) Score on the conservatism index, by state, 1972–1984. Calculated from *Congressional Quarterly*, 1972–1985.
   (f) Score on the innovation index, by state and occupation, 1972–1984. Calculated from Valletta and Freeman, 1985. The values reported where this variable is involved represent the mean correlation across the five occupations under study.

and deeply rooted political culture existing across the states. The strong positive relationship between income and expenditures per capita is to be expected. The link between urbanization and unionization fits the previous discussion as well. The two most surprising numbers in table 4.3 are the weak correlations between conservatism and urbanization ($-.20$) and between conservatism and per capita general expenditures (.00). The former correlation appears to confirm the finding of Faber and Martin that "urban" does not necessarily equate with "liberal." The latter figure seems to indicate that while a state might be predisposed toward an active role for government, it may be unwilling or unable to spend accordingly.

The strongest correlations in table 4.4 are between the policy measures and unionization, followed in magnitude by those with the scores on the conservatism and innovation scales. The weak levels of correlation between policy and urbanization, expenditures, and income per capita provide limited support for previous findings regarding their impact as policy-

Table 4.4
Intercorrelations Between Explanatory Variables and Policy Index Scores, By Occupation, 1972–1984

	EXPC	INPC	URBAN	ACADA	INNOV	UNION
State	.29	.24	.14	−.56	.63	.64
Police	.28	.27	.18	−.57	.51	.64
Fire	.29	.28	.15	−.50	.46	.47
Teachers	.25	.30	.18	−.58	.42	.55
Other Local	.25	.25	.14	−.58	.52	.64
All Occupations	.29	.28	.17	−.59	*n/a	.72

*Not applicable; innovation index calculated by occupation only.

determining factors. In the case of urbanization, the correlations presented here resemble those discovered by Faber and Martin for laws passed by 1975. Their figures were about half as strong for that year than they were for laws passed by 1968 (across both the interval and dichotomous measures of urbanization). It may be the case that the tailing off of the urban exodus during this period led to its decline as an explanation for policy. The weak correlations between policy and the economic measures cast doubt upon the vitality of Kochan's findings at an extended series of time points and with a more elaborate index of the law.

Next, the policy measures for each of the five occupations were regressed upon all six hypothesized antecedents on an annual basis (1972–1984) in order to gauge the joint effects of the latter over time.[5] The results of these operations appear in tables 4.5 through 4.9.

It is the high and relatively stable proportion of the variance explained by these models which first stands out in the tables. R-square ranges from .45 for firefighters in 1975 to .72 for state employees in 1980 and 1982. These models therefore explain a little less than half to almost three-quarters of the variation in cross-state bargaining policy, a consistent improvement upon those reported in Kochan's cross section.

In the context of occupational differences it is the four noneconomic measures which most often exhibit significant slope coefficients. For state employees the innovation and unionization indicators appear to provide

Table 4.5
Multiple Regression Results, By Year, Parameter Estimates: Policy Index Score Regressed Upon Explanatory Variables: State Employees

	Int.	EXPC	INPC	URBAN	ACADA	INNOV	UNION	R-SQ	F
1972	1.01	---	---	-.04 (.08)	-.02 (.03)	.34* (.11)	.11* (.05)	.47	6.38
1973	-1.10	.009@ (.005)	---	-.04 (.08)	-.02 (.03)	.46* (.12)	.09 (.05)	.55	8.78
1974	8.31	.004 (.005)	-.002 (.002)	-.05 (.08)	-.03 (.03)	.48* (.12)	.16* (.06)	.60	10.98
1975	7.84	.004 (.005)	-.001 (.002)	-.07 (.08)	-.04 (.03)	.47* (.12)	..16* (.06)	.63	12.27
1976	7.51	.002 (.006)	-.001 (.002)	-.05 (.10)	-.03 (.03)	.47* (.13)	.18* (.08)	.60	10.83
1977	6.39	.003 (.005)	---	-.08 (.10)	-.08* (.03)	.40* (.12)	.13@ (.07)	.65	13.27
1978	6.88	.001 (.005)	---	-.09 (.09)	-.05 (.04)	.42* (.11)	.20* (.07)	.66	13.66
1979	3.66	---	---	-.12 (.08)	-.04 (.03)	.43* (.10)	.21* (.05)	.70	16.97
1980	1.43	---	.001 (.001)	-.16* (.08)	-.05@ (.03)	.42* (.10)	.20* (.05)	.72	18.21
1981	.50	---	.001 (.001)	-.16* (.08)	-.04 (.03)	.47* (.10)	.21* (.05)	.71	17.39
1982	1.98	---	---	-.14@ (.08)	-.05@ (.03)	.45* (.10)	.19* (.05)	.72	18.06
1983	.98	---	---	-.14@ (.08)	-.04 (.03)	.45* (.10)	.21* (.05)	.71	17.42
1984	1.07	---	---	-.12 (.08)	-.04@ (.02)	.45* (.10)	.20* (.05)	.71	17.80

*p < .05
@p < .10
( ) = standard error
--- = coefficient < .001

the greatest explanatory power. These two variables and urbanization are most often significant for police and "other local" employees. Innovation and conservatism, respectively, receive the parameter estimates of greatest value in explaining policy for firefighters across the period of study.

Table 4.6
Multiple Regression Results, By Year, Parameter Estimates: Policy Index Score Regressed Upon Explanatory Variables: Police

	Int.	EXPC	INPC	URBAN	ACADA	INNOV	UNION	R-SQ	F
1972	7.23	-.005 (.004)	.002 (.002)	-.25* (.09)	-.05* (.02)	.10 (.10)	.24* (.06)	.63	12.07
1973	-.34	.005 (.004)	.003 (.002)	-.27* (.09)	-.03 (.02)	.29* (.10)	.21* (.06)	.67	14.38
1974	10.87	.004 (.005)	---	-.22@ (.11)	-.07* (.03)	.32* (.13)	.20* (.09)	.58	10.04
1975	3.75	.002 (.005)	.001 (.002)	-.19@ (.11)	-.06* (.02)	.33* (.13)	.16@ (.08)	.58	9.92
1976	8.32	-.001 (.005)	.001 (.002)	-.27* (.11)	-.04 (.03)	.30* (.13)	.26* (.08)	.62	11.79
1977	1.78	.001 (.005)	.002 (.002)	-.21@ (.11)	-.08* (.03)	.33* (.12)	.17* (.08)	.64	12.80
1978	-1.00	---	.002 (.002)	-.19@ (.11)	-.07@ (.04)	.31* (.13)	.19* (.08)	.63	12.19
1979	-3.12	---	.002 (.001)	-.24* (.11)	-.08* (.04)	.33* (.12)	.19* (.08)	.67	14.78
1980	-4.93	.001 (.002)	.002@ (.001)	-.24* (.10)	-.07@ (.04)	.26* (.12)	.21* (.08)	.69	15.84
1981	-3.58	.001 (.002)	.002 (.001)	-.28* (.10)	-.04 (.04)	.26@ (.13)	.25* (.07)	.66	14.10
1982	-4.63	---	.002@ (.001)	-.29* (.10)	-.03 (.03)	.25@ (.13)	.25* (.08)	.68	14.92
1983	-5.66	---	.002* (.001)	-.33* (.10)	---	.22@ (.13)	.30* (.07)	.67	14.87
1984	-3.77	.001 (.001)	.001@ (.001)	-.29* (.10)	-.01 (.03)	.21@ (.13)	.29* (.07)	.67	14.36

*p < .05
@p < .10
( ) = standard error
--- = coefficient < .001

Finally, it is the latter and unionization (i.e., beginning in about 1977) which appear to be most relevant to teachers.

There are a couple of surprises observable here. Consistent with the correlations, income and expenditures per capita possess less explanatory value than they do for Kochan's analysis. Much more counterintuitive

Table 4.7
Multiple Regression Results, By Year, Parameter Estimates: Policy Index Score
Regressed Upon Explanatory Variables: Firefighters

	Int.	EXPC	INPC	URBAN	ACADA	INNOV	UNION	R-SQ	F
1972	-4.10	-.003 (.005)	.004 (.002)	-.11 (.09)	-.07* (.03)	.23@ (.12)	.06 (.06)	.46	6.12
1973	-8.72	.010* (.004)	.003 (.002)	-.10 (.09)	-.06* (.03)	.30* (.13)	.02 (.06)	.53	8.20
1974	2.17	.008 (.006)	---	-.05 (.10)	-.10* (.03)	.22 (.15)	.03 (.08)	.46	6.20
1975	-3.80	.006 (.006)	.001 (.002)	-.07 (.10)	-.07* (.03)	.24 (.15)	.10 (.09)	.45	5.82
1976	-3.42	---	.002 (.002)	-.16 (.10)	-.07* (.03)	.31* (.14)	.15@ (.08)	.54	8.27
1977	-2.72	.002 (.005)	.001 (.002)	-.14 (.09)	-.08* (.03)	.38* (.13)	.16* (.07)	.59	10.38
1978	-7.12	.001 (.005)	.002 (.002)	-.11 (.10)	-.09* (.03)	.37* (.14)	.11 (.07)	.53	8.23
1979	-10.31	.001 (.003)	.002 (.001)	-.15 (.10)	-.10* (.03)	.38* (.14)	.11 (.06)	.58	9.93
1980	-10.78	.001 (.002)	.002@ (.001)	-.14 (.09)	-.10* (.03)	.37* (.14)	.07 (.06)	.56	9.15
1981	-8.61	.001 (.002)	.002 (.001)	-.14 (.10)	-.08* (.03)	.44* (.14)	.10 (.07)	.53	7.93
1982	-8.89	.001 (.002)	.002 (.001)	-.14 (.10)	-.08* (.03)	.42* (.14)	.09 (.06)	.54	8.36
1983	-14.36	---	.002@ (.001)	-.17 (.10)	-.04 (.03)	.41* (.15)	.14* (.06)	.50	7.08
1984	-14.07	---	.002@ (.001)	-.17 (.10)	-.04 (.03)	.37* (.15)	.15* (.06)	.50	7.21

*p < .05
@p < .10
( ) = standard error
--- = coefficient < .001

are the negative slopes associated with urbanization. The most plausible interpretation is that they might represent the unavoidable artifacts of data limits described earlier.

Overall, these more extensive tests provide stronger models of policy determination than do the two sets of patterns available previously. Var-

Table 4.8
Multiple Regression Results, By Year, Parameter Estimates: Policy Index Score
Regressed Upon Explanatory Variables: Teachers

	Int.	EXPC	INPC	URBAN	ACADA	INNOV	UNION	R-SQ	F
1972	-9.28	.002 (.004)	.005* (.002)	-.12 (.08)	-.09* (.02)	.15 (.12)	.04 (.07)	.56	9.21
1973	-13.66	.009* (.004)	.004* (.002)	-.07 (.07)	-.09* (.02)	.18 (.12)	.03 (.07)	.58	9.73
1974	-16.42	.004 (.005)	.003 (.002)	-.10 (.08)	-.09* (.02)	.19 (.14)	.17 (.11)	.54	8.51
1975	-19.01	.003 (.005)	.002 (.002)	-.10 (.08)	-.07* (.02)	.19 (.13)	.26* (.09)	.57	9.44
1976	-5.52	.003 (.005)	.001 (.002)	-.06 (.09)	-.10* (.02)	.21 (.15)	.10 (.10)	.51	7.50
1977	-7.98	.004 (.004)	.001 (.002)	-.05 (.09)	-.09* (.03)	.22 (.13)	.18* (.09)	.61	11.06
1978	-11.81	.002 (.004)	.001 (.001)	-.08 (.09)	-.08* (.04)	.23 (.14)	.20* (.09)	.56	8.99
1979	-9.26	-.002 (.003)	.001 (.001)	-.13 (.09)	-.07* (.03)	.21 (.14)	.28* (.08)	.60	10.57
1980	-13.23	-.001 (.002)	.002 (.001)	-.15@ (.08)	-.07* (.03)	.16 (.14)	.27* (.08)	.62	11.79
1981	-12.26	-.001 (.002)	.001 (.001)	-.14@ (.08)	-.06* (.03)	.19 (.13)	.29* (.08)	.62	11.86
1982	-11.59	---	.001 (.001)	-.14@ (.08)	-.06* (.02)	.18 (.13)	.29* (.08)	.63	12.22
1983	-17.45	-.001 (.001)	.001 (.001)	-.18* (.09)	-.03 (.03)	.17 (.14)	.35* (.07)	.61	11.25
1984	-15.91	-.001 (.001)	.001 (.001)	-.16@ (.09)	-.03 (.03)	.15 (.14)	.34* (.07)	.61	11.01

*p < .05
@p < .10
( ) = standard error
--- = coefficient < .001

iations therein across occupations indicate that answers to the antecedents
question may differ by category of the public payroll. Within functions,
however, the patterns remain relatively stable over time.

It is, of course, the manipulable variables which are of greatest substantive interest. The links between the policy and economic indicators

Table 4.9
Multiple Regression Results, By Year, Parameter Estimates: Policy Index Score Regressed Upon Explanatory Variables: Other Local Employees

	Int.	EXPC	INPC	URBAN	ACADA	INNOV	UNION	R-SQ	F
1972	6.08	-.008@ (.005)	.003 (.002)	-.22* (.09)	-.05 (.03)	.13 (.10)	.23* (.08)	.59	10.33
1973	-5.11	.005 (.005)	.003 (.002)	-.14 (.10)	-.06* (.03)	.22* (.11)	.13 (.08)	.59	10.45
1974	9.23	---	.001 (.002)	-.22* (.10)	-.07* (.03)	.19@ (.11)	.22* (.09)	.63	12.07
1975	6.60	-.003 (.006)	.002 (.002)	-.26* (.11)	-.05 (.03)	.20 (.12)	.26* (.10)	.59	10.39
1976	7.08	-.005 (.006)	.002 (.002)	-.24@ (.12)	-.06* (.03)	.26* (.13)	.21* (.09)	.59	10.11
1977	4.67	-.001 (.005)	.002 (.002)	-.19 (.12)	-.09* (.04)	.28* (.12)	.16 (.10)	.62	11.88
1978	6.27	-.005 (.006)	.002 (.002)	-.26* (.12)	-.06 (.04)	.27* (.12)	.25* (.10)	.60	10.85
1979	.68	-.003 (.004)	.002@ (.001)	-.27* (.13)	-.07@ (.04)	.33* (.12)	.19@ (.10)	.62	11.55
1980	-1.55	-.002 (.002)	.002* (.001)	-.28* (.12)	-.06 (.05)	.29* (.13)	.19@ (.10)	.62	11.53
1981	-.68	-.001 (.002)	.002@ (.001)	-.27* (.12)	-.05 (.04)	.34* (.14)	.21* (.09)	.62	11.47
1982	-1.46	-.001 (.002)	.001@ (.001)	-.26* (.12)	-.06 (.04)	.34* (.13)	.19@ (.10)	.63	12.23
1983	-2.31	-.002 (.002)	.002* (.001)	-.34* (.12)	-.01 (.04)	.27@ (.14)	.28* (.09)	.61	11.42
1984	-.71	-.001 (.001)	.002@ (.001)	-.29* (.12)	-.02 (.03)	.27@ (.14)	.25* (.09)	.61	11.16

*p < .05
@p < .10
(   ) = standard error
--- = coefficient < .001

are weak and those with urbanization unclear. Ideology (as assumed above) is durable over time and the innovation proxy adds little more than a measure of incrementalism to these tests. This leaves unionization as the sole candidate for a proactive policy recommendation. The message here would appear to be that, *ceteris paribus*, unions representing public employees can help themselves. The evidence suggests that recruitment efforts may bring not only the organizational benefits of a larger membership base but a more desirable policy climate as well, to the extent that size plays a role in the policy determination process.

What is obscured in this analysis, of course, is the fact that a unit change in the policy construct can mean the difference between whether, for example, strikes by any group of public employees are permitted (in some limited form) or receive no provision in the law. The nature of this indicator therefore prohibits any capacity to interpret the slope coefficients more concretely.

This fact complicates rather than negates the signals received here. These models consistently explain a substantial portion of the variance in policy. They also more fully test a general pattern of relationships which constitutes the balance of the accumulated knowledge about policy determination in this sphere.

DISCUSSION

Consistent with the essence of policy analysis, this chapter succeeds in mapping a portion of the theoretical terrain. The purpose of this analysis was to examine the vitality of our expectations, established by the previous (albeit limited) literature, about the origins of state public sector labor policy utilizing more complete policy data across other time points and occupations. We find:

1. Support for the "conventional wisdom" that more liberal (conservative) states are more (less) likely to institutionalize a collective bargaining relationship with their public employees.
2. Evidence to suggest that the additional suspects identified heretofore in the cumulative research—urbanization, income and expenditures per capita, innovation, and unionization—play a significant and reasonably consistent role in policy determination within and between the occupations studied.

A relatively strong inverse link between ideology and policy is observed across the period of observation. When alternative hypotheses are included in the model, a substantial proportion of the policy variance is explained. Measures of income and expenditure per capita play a weak antecedent role, and the pattern associated with urbanization is unclear. However, indicators employed for innovation and unionization, like ideology, show strong explanatory power. The significance of membership figures appears to contain some welcome news for the union-interested segment of the subnational public workforce. It provides room for optimism that these employees possess a degree of control over their collective fate.

Even so, the explanations for policy probed by this analysis remain inadequate. Clearer understanding of the unexplained portion of the variance is greatly inhibited by missing data. We may, of late, have a better idea about "what governments do," but the information required to test ideas about exogenous conditions as rigorously as might be preferred is lacking. Most constraining to the analysis pursued here was the fact that a longitudinal string of comparable state-level data on public sector union membership, disaggregated by occupation, could not be located prior to 1972 or after 1980. As will be observed momentarily, the absence of strike data of equal character necessary to test the relationship between policy and labor disruption limits our reach in a similar fashion.

The policy measure requires disaggregation as well. The ambiguity of the regression results presented above illustrates the need to think more in terms of specific provisions or identifiable "bundles" of policy. The goal, of course, is an ability to generalize, within the limits imposed by this style of comparative inquiry. With these things in mind, exploration of policy outcomes commences in chapter 5.

NOTES

1. For the purposes of this discussion, the term "ideology" is defined broadly to characterize the liberal or conservative nature of a state's population. Although typically interpreted more narrowly to describe consistently held belief systems at the individual level, this term seems to capture best the nature of the concept under study.

2. Note that the years cited by Faber and Martin are taken from a secondary source; the ratings they use actually correspond to ratings compiled by *CQ* for 1971, 1973, and 1975. On a separate point, these data become annual in 1965, the fourth time *CQ* published such ratings. The three previous observations correspond to ratings for each member in each of the three preceding biennial sessions of Congress (i.e., 1959–60, 1961–62, 1963–64).

3. For a concise discussion of the general quality of this indicator, see Barrilleaux and Miller, 1988, especially note 5, p. 1103.

4. Three methodological notes should be communicated explicitly before the analysis continues. The first involves Kochan's use of the Walker index as a measure of state innovation. Given the longitudinal nature of the regression analyses to come, the invariant composition of his scale is obviously problematic. In order to test the (competing) innovation hypothesis, a simple alternative proxy for this concept was constructed. The INNOV variable reported in tables 4.3 through 4.9 measures the time elapsed between the year under consideration and the year of first nonprohibitive policy adoption, by occupation. For example, Alabama authorized firefighters to present proposals in 1968; when policy for this group is considered in 1984, a score of sixteen is assigned. In other

words, the earlier the enactment, the longer the lapse, and the higher the score as time passes. Beyond the fact that it overcomes the variation problem, this measure on its face appears to provide policy-specific information (i.e., on earlier or later adoption, and therefore on the age of policy) not contained in Walker's more general index. (For a good overview of the positive and negative implications associated with this strategy, see Schneider, 1982, p. 7). The second issue relates to Kochan's use of a change measure for income per capita. The INPC variable is annual in this analysis, for the same reason that Walker's index was replaced. Finally, it should be noted as well that the substitute (i.e., Valletta and Freeman) 1972 policy scores were regressed upon these two and the expenditures per capita (EXPC) variable in order to replicate his findings as a baseline. The magnitude of the slope coefficients and the R-square were consistent with his results.

5. The period studied unfortunately reflects something of a "mix-and-match" strategy, unavoidable given the serious data limitations by which analysts of public sector bargaining find themselves constrained. The unionization variable was a primary consideration here. The disaggregated Census data do not begin until 1972, skip 1973, and end in 1980. The 1972 data are carried over to 1973 and the 1980 data are therefore employed in the last five cross sections (1980–1984), given (1) no substitute, and (2) the availability of the other five variables. Complete policy data end in 1984. The only other exceptions to annual figures are the urbanization measures, which are inextricably tied to the decennial census. The 1970 and 1980 figures are used throughout each decade, respectively.

5 What Difference It Makes:
The Impacts of Policy

The research thus far has been framed around two central ideas: first, that there are potential benefits to be realized from bilateralism in the public workplace, and, second, that the political process can suffer if the pendulum of power is suspended at labor's side of its arc through policy. As suggested in the introduction, it is balance which is sought by policymakers. To the extent that they are interested in collective bargaining, they hope to institutionalize co-determination without pathology.

Subnational decision makers need to know two things. They need to know whether their actions will foster or impede collective activity: unionization is a necessary condition for bargaining to occur. They also need to know how to avoid, at the extreme, the service disruption which can place their budgetary and procedural authority at risk.

The task of sorting out these issues is an imposing one. Although the link between scholarship and policymaking is at best tenuous, the limited nature of research efforts to date means that policy analysts offer those charged with making these public decisions very little information about the results of the policy experimentation in which they have been engaged. The reappearance of the unionization variable in this chapter shows that the question of whether policy drives union growth or is driven by it is an open one. Worse, difficulties in modeling strikes (to be discussed in a moment) means that methods which can be employed to avoid them remain in doubt.

This third analytical chapter attempts to shed greater light upon outcomes. Here policy becomes the independent variable. The concerns expressed above mean that two dependent variables are key on the left side of the equation: union growth and service disruption.

THE LITERATURE

Union Growth

Unlike most other dimensions of the literature, the consistent finding across a handful of published empirical studies is that the configuration of state labor law matters; unions prosper as policy becomes more progressive and comprehensive. In what appears to be the earliest treatment of unionism in the public sector, William Moore (1977) attempts to explain cross-state variation in public sector union membership with a model adapted from a previous study of the private sector (Moore and Newman, 1975). Using discriminant analysis to construct a policy variable capable of distinguishing nonadopters from those states enacting comprehensive or permissive bargaining statutes, Moore finds that this variable, two demographic factors (i.e., the racial and age composition of the workforce), and urbanization explain over half the variance of the dependent variable. Yet data limitations once again constrain the vitality of his conclusion, as he is forced to regress a 1968 cross section of unionization upon a 1970 measure of policy. Though he contends in a footnote that radical change in the dependent variable is not expected, this problem of temporal precedence is exacerbated if (1) policy is rapidly changing, and (2) a lag between adoption and impact can be expected. Both would appear to be true for this period of legal development.

In a subsequent analysis, Moore (1978) examines fluctuations in union membership among teachers cross sectionally and over time. His time series results (1919–1970) indicate that changes in AFT and NEA membership are unrelated to policy when a host of alternative explanations are considered in the model. However, the results for a 1970 cross section of membership and contract data lend marginal support (p slightly $>$ .10 for one of two policy dummies) to the policy-unionization hypothesis. His conclusion is that mandatory bargaining laws help the AFT but not the NEA.

This finding receives further support in the work of Amy Dalton (1982). She uses two-stage least squares estimates to explain the variance in unionization across state and local governments and six specific government functions in 1977. Her dummy variable for mandatory bargaining policy appears to matter in all cases, as do the size of government and the degree of unionization in the private sector labor force.[1]

Jim Seroka (1985) attempts the most ambitious study of public sector union growth in the literature. He disaggregates by eight functional occupations and five levels of government for the 1972–1980 period. Building upon the work of his predecessors, he hypothesizes that growth is a function of policy (operationalized this time as a four-point Guttman scale), unemployment, change in per capita income, political ideology, government expenditures, the magnitude of unionization in the private sector, and the size of the public workforce. His result contains both good news and bad: policy appears to make the strongest contribution to the variance explained by the model, but it is only policy that is consistent in impact. All other variables have differential or negligible effects. The implication is that what policymakers do makes a difference, but that the efficacy of their actions may vary by government and function.

Service Disruption

Scholars devote more ink to empirical studies of public sector strikes. This is no real surprise, given the usual fears about union power. The most consistent result appears to be that policy plays a significant role here as well, although about a third of the research output finds the opposite. To be more specific, it appears that a combination of third-party procedures (particularly compulsory arbitration), strike provisions, and bargaining rights reduces the number of strikes faced by a subnational jurisdiction.

The seminal (and arguably most rigorous) piece on public sector strikes establishes the minority view (Burton and Krider, 1975). Deriving their theory of government-specific disruption from an exhaustive review of the relevant industrial relations research, the authors test their hypotheses cross-state for a three-year period (1968 1971). They regress data describing the incidence of strikes in the local government, noneducation sector upon three categories of determinants: statutory provisions, the unionization of public employees, and significant economic, political, and sociological characteristics of the state environment. They find that policy has no impact, nor do many of the other indicators show consistent effects; "the simplest explanation," they conclude, "is that most public-sector strike activity is unpredictable" (p. 171).

If an interesting research question was not enough to justify additional effort, this counterintuitive finding made the issue even more compelling.[2] The result was a host of new analyses varying across three dimensions: model specification, unit of analysis, and time point or period.

Hoyt Wheeler (1975) was one of the first to locate evidence suggesting a different conclusion. Working at approximately the same time as Burton and Krider with preliminary BLS data, Wheeler's quick cross-tabulation of firefighter strikes by impasse law (selected U.S. cities, 1969–1972) finds none where arbitration is compulsory.[3] Four subsequent studies of teachers yield similar generalizations about policy. Weintraub and Thornton (1976) find that between 1946 and 1973, school districts with permissive bargaining legislation suffer fewer strikes than their counterparts without it (though a high level of colinearity—R-squared as high as .97—inhibits their ability to estimate the independent effects of exogenous indicators). Two studies by Horn, McGuire, and Tomkiewicz (1982a, 1982b) reach comparable conclusions; TOBIT estimation of teacher strikes in a 1977 cross section and for a 1975–1978 pool indicate that districts which encourage collective bargaining incur less disruption than those operating within meet-and-confer frameworks or those with no law. The last of the four (Balfour and Holmes, 1981) hypothesizes and finds statistical evidence of a parabolic relationship between strike policy and disruption. Strikes are most frequent when permitted or heavily sanctioned, least frequent in those states with moderate penalties (time period: 1974–77).

The only teacher-specific analysis finding no apparent covariation between policy and disruption was that performed by Colton (1978). He finds that the incidence of strikes remained unchanged or marginally decreased in a majority of states adopting collective bargaining statutes between 1960 and 1975. He attributes post-adoption increases occurring in the minority to regional differences in political culture, within-region (i.e., nonpolicy) variation, and other social forces (e.g., the general unrest of the late 1960s).

The final cluster of empirical contributions to this literature examines policy impacts across alternative occupations, a specific state, and/or wider time periods. Ichniowski (1982) concentrates his effort on municipal police departments. His time series estimates (1972–1973, 1976–1978) support the generalization that compulsory arbitration decreases the probability that strikes will occur. He further informs his analysis with a series of interviews in the handful of cities experiencing disruption regardless of an available arbitration mechanism. The conclusion: delays in the dispute-resolution process and frustration with the time elapsed since contract expiration appear to be responsible.[4]

Stern and Olson (1982) achieve similar results for police, teacher, and firefighter strikes between 1975 and 1977. They find that any group's propensity to strike during negotiations (a new configuration of the dependent variable) is consistently lowest under mandatory arbitration, and highest when there is no law on the books.

Klauser's (1977) case study of Hawaii provides a final clue about the impact of subnational labor policy. He observes only one (two-week) strike across fifty-one agreements negotiated during the seven years following passage of the Hawaii Public Employment Relations Act (1970). He attributes this peace to legalization (i.e., strikes permitted, with qualifications, following mediation, fact-finding, and voluntary arbitration), though he does recognize that Hawaii's geographic isolation, its political structure, and the broad "public health and safety" charge of its PERB may have influence as well.

Summary

Though somewhat inconsistent, the weight of the evidence suggests that policy plays a determining role in union growth and in service disruption. In the case of the former, it does indeed appear (congruent with Freeman's assertion in chapter 2) that unions prosper in a sympathetic environment. Policy decisions about bargaining rights, arbitration, and strikes seem to affect the frequency of the latter.

There are some bothersome gaps left to fill, however. For example, if the recommendation to policymakers interested in unionization among their public employees is that it is enhanced when they establish a permissive or progressive bargaining environment, what specific components does such an environment entail? Prescriptions about disruption come from something of an opposite direction. The accumulated wisdom here suggests to legislators that permissive bargaining rights, compulsory arbitration, and various configurations of strike policy are useful inhibitors, with the caveat that the bulk of this knowledge comes from analyses of teachers at varied time points.

Two new research questions emerge from this perspective on the literature:

1. What specific policy measures affect collective action among public employees?
2. Do conclusions about the relationship between policy and disruption hold up across a wider set of occupations, jurisdictions, and time points?

Exploration of both constitutes the focus of this chapter.

FURTHER TESTING

Although the Valletta and Freeman data enhanced the picture of policy available (they are used again below), this piece of luck does not extend to the search for a longitudinal string of comparable data describing unionization and disruption in subnational jurisdictions. Analysts have been forced to rely heavily upon the Bureau of the Census for the widest view of these dependent variables across the states and localities. Probably because state legislative action was sporadic until the late 1960s, the Census did not begin regular, comprehensive reporting of (their own and BLS) statistics until 1972; budgetary cutbacks during Ronald Reagan's first term severely restricted the collection effort by 1982.[5]

Apparently only Felker (1986) attempts to utilize the entire string of outcome data to model both dependent variables. Employing a "modified" version of a legislation scale developed by Hopkins, Rawson, and Smith (1976), Felker examines relationships between this policy indicator, labor organization membership, and conflict. He finds moderate covariation between the policy environment and unionization, but correlations between the former and his disruption measures are quite weak. His conclusion is that while legislative action is strongly linked to patterns of organization, it appears to have few of the disastrous consequences typically associated with collective bargaining in the public sector.

Felker's analysis speaks to only a portion of each research question above, however. His modified policy indicator (exact specification unknown) would appear to measure only the "permissiveness" dimension of the statutory environment, thereby neglecting the impact of alternative policy actors and leaving open the question of specific provisions. The fact that he does not disaggregate by occupation means that further testing is merited here as well. His second finding is particularly intriguing; that it contradicts the more recent work makes this lack of covariation curious.

The first step toward reexamining the data is to replicate Felker's analysis with a known policy measure. Given the ambiguity of his policy variable, the goal is to determine the degree to which his weak correlations (particularly with the disruption indicators) are the result of specification problems. Additional goals are (1) to disaggregate the relationships by functional occupation and by year, and (2) to test the necessity for various lagged models.

Three sets of dependent variables are employed in this portion of the analysis. Union membership is measured once again as the percentage of full-time employees organized. Four disruption indicators were extracted from the Census data: the number of strikes,[6] the number of employees involved, strike duration, and the number of days idle (i.e., number of employees times duration). The third category of data contains five indicators designed to measure the diffusion of bargaining in any state: the number of bargaining units, the number and proportion of all governments with one or more bargaining units, and the number and

Table 5.1
Intercorrelations, By Year, State Policy With Unionization and Disruption Indicators, 1972, 1974–1980, 1982

Year	% Union	Strikes	Employees Involved	Duration	Days Idle
1972	.73	.25	.36	.26	-.18
1974	.71	.16	.07	.18	.07
1975	.71	.18	.18	.19	.16
1976	.68	.07	.20	.10	.13
1977	.71	.15	.15	.21	.15
1978	.74	.10	.05	.13	-.02
1979	.76	.09	.12	.09	.10
1980	.77	.10	.07	.14	.07
1982	.75	*n/a	*n/a	*n/a	*n/a
All Years	.71	.13	.13	.16	.10

Not applicable; disruption data unavailable.

proportion of all governments engaging in collective negotiations. The data were collected on a total state and local basis (where applicable), and across the same five occupations used in chapters 3 and 4 for 1972, 1974–1980, and 1982. (n = 450 for the aggregate-level data set, n = 2000 for the disaggregation.)

The NBER data are employed for a third time as the substitute policy indicator. Note that the use of these data in the analysis to follow requires that their structure be considered carefully. Critical problems and fixes associated with the ways in which these data are manipulated are discussed in appendix 5.1, located at the end of this chapter.

Table 5.1 reports the correlations between policy, unionization, and the four disruption indicators, disaggregated by year across all observations. The coefficients resemble those reported by Felker in sign and magnitude, though the level of covariation between policy and unionization is a good deal stronger with the new measure of the former. It would appear that the organization of public employees has a strong (and relatively stable) relationship to the legal environment of bargaining, and that either (1) policy has only weak ties to disruption (Felker's interpretation), or (2) it is a more complex phenomenon not modeled adequately with a testing strategy such as this one.

Table 5.2 examines the simple correlations between policy and the

Table 5.2
Intercorrelations, By Year, State Policy With Diffusion Indicators, 1972, 1974–1980, 1982

Year	No. of Bargaining Units	No. Gov'ts With 1+ Units	% All Gov'ts	No. Gov'ts With Coll. Negotiations	% All Gov'ts
1972	*n/a	*n/a	*n/a	.41	.70
1974	.34	.30	.57	.39	.63
1975	.35	.29	.58	.38	.65
1976	.33	.26	.63	.35	.69
1977	.37	.33	.71	.38	.74
1978	.39	.35	.70	.40	.74
1979	.39	.35	.71	.39	.75
1980	.38	.34	.71	.38	.75
1982	.40	.36	.73	.40	.76
All Years	.37	.33	.67	.40	.72

Not applicable; diffusion data unavailable.

augmented measures of bargaining diffusion at the state level. Like union growth, the theoretically appealing interpretation is that the spread of bargaining relationships increases as the policy environment becomes more structured. Though here, too, causation cannot be established with a correlation (making this statistic worthless in the view of some analysts), it is unlikely that local governments would implement procedures for unit determination little more than sporadically absent state-level encouragement. (The strong and stable associations that emerge when the number of governments is controlled in the functional form of this "dependent" variable also lend support to the assumption employed as a fix for the third problem identified in appendix 5.1).

Table 5.3 returns to the primary focus and disaggregates the policy-unionization and policy-disruption coefficients by occupation. Most interesting here is the change in sign associated with the weak correlations for the latter in the cases of police and firefighters. The intuitive explanation would seem to be that policy succeeds at being more strike-averse for these two groups of public safety employees. It was suggested in the earlier discussion (chapters 1 and 3) that state and local legislators generally regulate their uniformed services more closely than they do others. Their actions make some margin of difference, if these correlations are any gauge; the alternative hypothesis that increased disruption results in

Table 5.3
Intercorrelations, By Occupation, State Policy With Unionization and Disruption Indicators, 1972, 1974–1980

Occupation	% Union	Strikes	Employees Involved	Duration	Days Idle
State	.63	.21	.14	.12	.15
Police	.62	-.10	-.06	-.08	-.04
Fire	.47	-.16	-.12	-.13	-.07
Teachers	.51	.17	.11	.18	.09
Other Local	.63	.13	.11	.17	.10

a less structured environment makes much less sense. Regardless, the weak associations indicate that there is much more at work here than can be assessed with this analytical approach.[7]

Up to this point only crude structural differences across state bargaining environments have been examined. More compelling is the need to think about specific policy provisions and to get a better handle on the disruption data.

Table 5.4 contains the results from a factor analysis (varimax rotation) of the policy measures. One intent is to determine the degree to which specific bargaining provisions are "bundled" by policymakers. Though statistically suspect (see appendix 5.1), this procedure makes much more theoretical sense than a multitude of distinct dummy variables or than considering policy impacts (the second rationale) one provision at a time.

It appears from this operation that policy actors make three relatively distinct sets of decisions. Factor 1 might be best labeled "basic rights" policy, as it contains those provisions most essential to the establishment of a minimally viable bargaining relationship (i.e., duty of the employer, unit determination, and so forth). As might be expected, the arbitration dimensions load on a common factor (factor 2), though arguments about its particular importance to the public sector might lead to a prediction of higher loadings on the first (as with strike policy, below). Factor 3 contains those elements most significant to union security.[8]

Three additional dimensions of table 5.4 stand out. First, the prevalence of uniform union and agency shop prohibitions in the Right-to-Work states means that factor 3 is probably best called "union *in*security." Similarly, the fact that on average 68 percent of the states specifically prohibit strikes (with or without explicit penalties) by 1984 helps to explain the loading of this variable here as well.[9] Finally, although dues

Table 5.4
Rotated Factor Pattern, State Policy Data, 1972, 1974–1980

Policy Dimension	Factor 1	Factor 2	Factor 3
Bargaining Rights	.89	.25	.06
Scope of Bargaining	.84	.24	.04
Representation/Election	.92	.28	.06
Term of Recognition	.78	.29	.06
Mediation: Availability	.81	.26	.00
Fact-finding: Availability	.78	.01	-.11
Arbitration: Availability	.37	.81	.00
Arbitration: Scope	.26	.91	.04
Arbitration: Type	.17	.91	.00
Union Shop	-.07	-.07	.82
Agency Shop	.43	.25	.64
Right-to-Work Law	.20	.09	.81
Strike Policy	-.20	-.06	.61
Dues Checkoff	.40	.31	.08

checkoff might be expected to load with the other union security provisions, its weak distribution across the factors also makes sense given the low cost of this concession to the employer (elaborated in chapter 3).

The next step is to regress the dependent variables upon the scored policy data in order to make better sense of the bivariate relationships. This procedure turns out to be spectacularly unsuccessful for the disruption indicators—policy explains only about 3 percent of the variance. (These data are reexamined momentarily.) There is solace to be taken, however, from somewhat better results for union growth. The standardized parameter estimates for these equations appear in table 5.5, disaggregated by occupation on an annual basis.[10]

Although coefficients vary across time and function, policy appears to be a determinant of union growth. It regularly explains about one-quarter to one-half of the variance across cases, and as much as 64 percent of police organization in 1978. The basic policy and arbitration factors appear to be the major contributors across occupations, yet the insecurity dimension is significant for state and other local employees over the course of the period (although of counterintuitive sign). Coefficients for the latter are also smallest for police, firefighters, and teachers. This is surprising

Table 5.5
Multiple Regression Results, By Occupation and Year, Standardized Parameter Estimates: Unionization Regressed Upon Three Policy Factors, 1972, 1974–1980

Occ.	Exogenous Variable	1972	1974	1975	1976	1977	1978	1979	1980
State	Factor 1	.44*	.50*	.47*	.51*	.56*	.61*	.66*	.68*
	Factor 2	.13	.22@	.28*	.26*	.18@	.23*	.20*	.16
	Factor 3	.25@	.31*	.32*	.30*	.34*	.34*	.29*	.25*
	R-square	.28	.40	.40	.41	.46	.54	.56	.54
	F	5.83	10.02	10.33	10.80	13.18	17.75	19.81	18.25
Police	Factor 1	.58*	.38*	.35*	.36*	.34*	.30*	.31*	.35*
	Factor 2	.31*	.40*	.49*	.59*	.60*	.73*	.70*	.71*
	Factor 3	.19@	.18	.11	.15	.12	.15@	.12	.10
	R-square	.47	.34	.37	.49	.49	.64	.61	.63
	F	13.58	7.97	9.19	14.84	14.63	27.66	23.63	26.30
Fire	Factor 1	.34*	.17	.20	.28*	.32*	.23*	.22@	.21@
	Factor 2	.35*	.37*	.50*	.52*	.53*	.58*	.57*	.58*
	Factor 3	-.04	.04	.05	.00	.06	.04	.00	-.03
	R-square	.24	.16	.29	.35	.39	.39	.37	.38
	F	4.74	3.03	6.22	8.24	9.72	9.97	9.14	9.48
Teachers	Factor 1	.13	.31*	.41*	.26*	.56*	.52*	.60*	.62*
	Factor 2	.15	.31*	.37*	.35*	.37*	.42*	.39*	.37*
	Factor 3	-.02	-.05	.03	.17	.12	.16	.13	.13
	R-square	.04	.20	.31	.23	.47	.48	.53	.54
	F	.66	3.73	6.90	4.46	13.34	13.92	17.32	17.69
Other Local	Factor 1	.67*	.61*	.61*	.57*	.59*	.59*	.54*	.57*
	Factor 2	.13	.11	.06	.12	.13	.17	.23*	.22@
	Factor 3	.16	.26*	.26*	.28*	.27*	.32*	.31*	.31*
	R-square	.49	.45	.45	.42	.44	.48	.45	.46
	F	14.49	12.71	12.33	10.98	12.00	14.15	12.30	13.24

*p < .05
@p < .10

when the theoretical importance attached to this category of provisions is considered.

These results suggest two things. They substantiate earlier conclusions about the link between policy and union membership. In particular, they provide greater confidence that the organizing efforts of public employees are positively related to a structure of basic bargaining rights and third-party procedures. Second, differentials among the estimates support Seroka's evidence (above) that generalizations may be limited by occupation and/or time point. Both conclusions are tentative, of course, as they require further examination in light of appropriate controls and competing hypotheses about causation.

The relationship between policy and disruption (or to be more accurate, the apparent lack of one in these data) is the more immediate concern. The final segment of the analysis explores this issue further.

Felker's analysis and the initial attempts to replicate and to disaggregate above make it appear that disruption has very little relationship to the policy environment. The literature and basic presumptions about the significance of politics and policymaking lead to the opposite expectation. Rather than prematurely accepting the conclusion that there is no covariation between the two, the possibility that Felker overlooked an alternative hypothesis—specification error—must be considered. A closer look at data and approach is therefore in order.

The apparent solutions to the riddle can be provided up front. The first relates to an idea set forth in chapter 2 about the dimensionality of the labor-management relationships established through policy action. It was suggested there that one dimension encompasses the necessary preconditions for bilateralism. For example, employees must organize and choose their leadership before they can negotiate or strike because of impasse or grievance. Another dimension corresponds to the ongoing character of the relationship itself (e.g., its harmony or conflict) once labor representation is in place. The point is that the necessary conditions appear to form an intervening variable between policy and outcome, which may account for the marginal covariation found in the aggregate data. This is not, however, a tidy linear progression of successive steps (i.e., policy → relationship → level of disruption). For example, unorganized workers can and sometimes do band together (often with the help of a union entrepreneur) to seek representational rights where policy is prohibitive (e.g., policy → disruption → relationship) or where it is silent (e.g., disruption → policy → relationship).[11]

The second solution is most visible in the disaggregated data. At any time point, the probability that a strike will *not* occur is higher than the probability that a strike will take place. This makes sense (given multiyear contracts, for example) and it is reassuring to policymakers. However, it does garble the signals transmitted by statistical estimates of covariation. From a simple PRE (proportional reduction of error) perspective, it can appear that knowing the independent variable is unhelpful when in fact systematic differences do exist across the attributes of the exogenous

Table 5.6
Intercorrelations Between Diffusion and Disruption Indicators, 1972, 1974–1980

Disruption Variable	No. of Bargaining Units	No. Gov'ts With 1+ Units	% All Gov'ts	No. Gov'ts With Coll. Negotiations	% All Gov'ts
Strikes	.71	.76	.37	.74	.34
Employees Involved	.64	.66	.32	.64	.30
Duration	.60	.69	.26	.68	.24
Days Idle	.61	.64	.27	.59	.23

indicator. A type II inference error results; the null hypothesis is accepted by mistake.

Table 5.6 speaks to the first set of ideas. Correlations between the diffusion and disruption measures indicate strong relationships between the latter and the number of bargaining units, the number of governments with one or more bargaining units, and the number engaging in collective negotiations. When the number of governments is controlled (i.e., the percentage variables) the correlations are reduced by about half, no particular surprise in that (1) the two forms of the diffusion variable are measuring different shades of bargaining scope (i.e., spread across jurisdictions vs. the number of specific leverage points), and (2) its variance is constrained when transformed in this fashion.

Evidence presented earlier in this chapter showed strong covariation between policy and diffusion. Here strong relationships between diffusion and disruption are observed.[12] Taken together, these results lend support to an intervening variable argument.

Table 5.7 contains findings relevant to the statistical issue, the final piece of the puzzle to be presented here. Column A lists each category of policy found to be significant in the literature, disaggregated by provision. Column B reports the incidence of each provision, that is, the number of times across the period in which the provision is in force for any occupation. Column C presents strike frequencies.

The most interesting dimension of column C is the large number of strikes that fall in the more permissive categories of policy. For example, almost two-thirds of all strikes occur in those jurisdictions that make the employer's duty to bargain either implied or explicit. A proportion of similar magnitude appears for those cases in which strikes are either

Table 5.7
Strike Frequencies By Selected Policy Provisions, 1972, 1974–1980

Policy Variable	N ( ) = %	Strikes ( ) = %	Strikes/ Adoption	1+ Strikes	No Strike	p
(A)	(B)	(C)	(D)	(E)	(F)	(G)
Bargaining Rights:						
No Provision	383 (19.1)	772 (15.2)	2.02	141	242	.37
Prohibited	143 (7.1)	161 (3.2)	1.13	50	93	.35
Authorized	354 (17.7)	728 (14.3)	2.06	136	218	.38
Proposals	48 (2.4)	10 (0.2)	0.21	8	40	.17
Meet and Confer	81 (4.0)	147 (6.7)	1.81	40	41	.49
Duty Implied	784 (39.2)	2197 (43.2)	2.80	314	470	.40
Duty Explicit	207 (10.3)	1075 (21.1)	5.19	96	111	.46
Strike Policy:						
No Provision	558 (27.9)	783 (15.4)	1.40	211	347	.38
Penalties	504 (25.2)	1114 (21.9)	2.21	164	340	.33
No Penalties	777 (38.9)	2152 (42.3)	2.77	326	451	.42
Permitted	161 (8.0)	1041 (20.5)	6.47	84	77	.52
Arbitration:						
No Provision	1323 (66.2)	3009 (59.1)	2.27	505	818	.38
Prohibited	8 (0.4)	49 (1.0)	6.12	4	4	.50
Voluntary	359 (18.0)	1819 (35.7)	5.07	191	168	.53
Discretionary	191 (9.6)	142 (2.8)	0.74	53	138	.28
Mandatory	119 (6.0)	71 (1.4)	0.60	32	87	.27

prohibited without penalties or permitted with qualifications. It would seem that strikes are a price of collective bargaining.

What is bothersome about columns B and C is the degree to which the percentages correspond. If strikes fall in direct proportion to the incidence of each provision, odds of 1:1 result in each category, and thus no relationship exists between the variables. This means that differences between the categories should be examined while the frequency of adoption is controlled.

Column D goes part of the way by figuring the number of strikes that occur per incidence of any provision (C divided by B). Differences become much more apparent. Most notable are the results associated with an explicit employer duty, "legalized" strikes, and discretionary or mandatory arbitration. In the case of the first two, the price of bargaining is reaffirmed. The bottom of column D also suggests many fewer strikes when arbitration is used, either because it is easy to do so when discretionary or because parties to an impasse have no choice.

These data can be transformed into strike probabilities across states, time points, and occupations as well. By collapsing the data into a strike-no strike dichotomy by incidence of provision (columns E and F), the probability (p) that one or more strikes will occur, given the incidence of a specific provision, can be calculated (column G). Looking at columns E and F from the perspective of lambda (to treat the data as nominal for a moment), the PRE interpretation suggested above can be observed. Correlations are nonexistent because ''no strike'' is always predicted even when the hypothesized independent variable is known. This situation leads to the anticipated type II error.

However, column G (E divided by B) provides evidence to the contrary.[13] In the case of bargaining rights, the differences are not dramatic, but they do tend to indicate something of a bimodal strike propensity. It would appear from these data that strikes are likely about one-third of the time when the employer's duty to bargain is weak or nonexistent. Strikes seem somewhat more likely as the employer's obligation becomes more compelling.

A second indication is that higher strike probabilities are associated with permissive strike policy. The data say nothing about when or what sanctions are actually applied, significant issues. As suggested by these findings, however, the bias would seem to be against lenient policy if the priority is to minimize disruption.

The arbitration results are the most dramatic, but they are not unexpected. The signal here is that arbitration pays off. Strike probabilities are much smaller where arbitration has a realistic chance of being utilized; that is, the p value drops dramatically to nearly half its previous magnitude when arbitration is discretionary (i.e., one-party consent) or mandatory. Under the other three provisions arbitration is either not an option (i.e., no provision, prohibited) or it is not likely to be used often (i.e., the voluntary case, in which two-party consent is required). There is a relationship between policy and disruption, if these bivariate findings are any guide.

DISCUSSION

Subnational policymakers recognize the benefits and pitfalls which can be associated with collective bargaining in their jurisdictions. They typically face a tradeoff between the advantages of an organized workforce and the political costs of the strike. What they need to know is how to maximize the former and how to minimize the latter.

These are interesting questions for social scientists in general and for political scientists in particular. The policy analysts among them have the goal and the virtue of trying to reduce the uncertainty faced by the policymaker. This is easier said than done. Limited data of multiple dimensions mean that those doing research in this sphere must juggle many balls simultaneously.

Difficulties associated with establishing the relevant linkages in this area are reflected in the literature. Though few balls are dropped, concentration on one limits their ability to deal with others. What emerges are mixed and limited signals about the general phenomenon of collective bargaining in the public sector, if there are indeed generalizations to be made across time points, jurisdictions, and occupations.

This chapter contains an effort to replicate, to synthesize, and to explore this set of relationships further. It presents evidence suggesting that:

1. Policymakers make three sets of decisions. They seem to develop a system of basic collective bargaining rights, they consider union security issues, and they pay special attention to arbitration.

2. A reasonably strong link exists between policy and union membership, particularly in terms of the variance explained in the latter by the rights and arbitration factors.

3. A more complex relationship exists between policy and service disruption. Policy appears to have an important relationship to the diffusion of bargaining, to which in turn the frequency of disruption may be tied.

4. A direct link exists between policy and disruption as well. The latter covaries with the degree of the public employer's obligation, the treatment of strikes, and the availability of arbitration;

5. Changing or different relationships exist between occupations and over time.

These are interesting results, for they provide an indication that subnational policymakers possess a set of levers through which the collective bargaining process can be regulated. This possibility should be of interest to subnational officials who are often quite concerned about maintaining their managerial autonomy in the face of high-pressure union demands. The broad implication, of course, is that the skill they demonstrate in using these tools will have significant impact upon the integrity of pluralist politics within their jurisdictions. More will be said about this issue in the next chapter.

The need for further testing is obvious. Two dimensions are most compelling. First, causation remains a significant unknown. Bivariate correlations often play an important role in the mapping process, as they do here. Even so, more sophisticated techniques must be employed in new analyses if the direction of these and other links is to be firmly grounded.

Second, quasiexperimentation requires that alternative hypotheses be eliminated if the effects of the policy variables are to be isolated and before causation is attributable. As can be observed in the work here, theory provides only limited assistance in interpreting the empirical results. Once the direct policy-outcome linkages become more tangible, the impacts of appropriate control variables can be gauged as well. These issues and other questions unearthed by this research constitute an important agenda for the future. Specific ideas about the shape of that agenda are discussed in chapter 6.

NOTES

1. For a hearty argument about her design choices, see the objections of Reid and Kurth (1984) and Dalton (1984) for her response.

2. It is also reminiscent of the early comparative state politics literature. In that case it was the "nonfindings" of Dawson and Robinson (1963), Dye (1966), Hofferbert (1966; 1968), and others which led to the long-standing (some say long-winded) debate over politics vs. economics among political scientists.

3. Both Burton-Krider and Wheeler were quickly contradicted as well. Rodgers (1980) replicates the former with 1974–75 data to reach opposite conclusions about strike provisions and third-party procedures. Fallon (1977) examines data on public sector strikes in 1972 to find that mandatory arbitration has no impact. The latter apparently remains unpublished, and both were unavailable to the author at the time this was written. See Freeman, 1986, pp. 67–70, for details.

4. The short nationwide rail strike of April 1991 appears to fit this generalization precisely. At least according to the media, both variables were cited by the relevant participants as its central causes.

5. The data referred to here and used below are found in two places: (a) in the *Census of Governments* (U.S. Department of Commerce, 1972; 1977; 1982), and (b) in that series of special studies by the Bureau of the Census used in chapter 4 (U.S. Department of Commerce, 1974–1976; 1978–1980).

6. Estimating this parameter became something of a problem when constructing observations for "other local" employees. Census reports the number of strikes that occur, regardless of the number of occupations involved. As one strike by one occupation is arguably less severe than a concurrent strike by two or more, the final configuration of the variable for this group of employees represents the number of occupations other than police, fire, and teaching on strike at any time point. This overstates the actual number of strikes associated with "other local" occupations, but a series of subsequent tests in which this category was omitted showed only negligible changes in results.

7. Two final notes before we proceed. First, lags become fairly immediate suspects in cases of weak association. Policy lags of one, two, and three years led to insignificant changes in the sign and magnitude of the coefficients. If anything, they were remarkably stable. These operations were performed with the disaggregated data, which were analyzed in the fashion indicated by the tables. Second, table 5.3 is a fair representation of the relevant correlation in any year, so the annual results are omitted for ease of presentation.

8. Once again the output is not disaggregated in order to facilitate presentation. Even

so, the communication of temporal and occupational deviations from this pattern is warranted. First it should be noted that in 1972 the factor analytic operation (after rotation) results in a four-factor solution across each of the occupations. Three emerge consistently for state, police, and other local employees beginning in 1974. The generalization with respect to the firefighter data is the same; the only exception is an outcome of four factors in 1975. Policy covering teachers is the outlier: only in 1977 and 1980 are three rather than four factors constructed. In order to perform fair and useful testing below, the NFACTORS = 3 option in SAS was employed. A consistent set of patterns true to table 5.4 resulted. The second set of notable variations corresponds to the loadings of the strike and dues measures in this context. Though all other loadings are quite stable, the strike indicator jumps back and forth a bit between factors 1 and 3. Dues checkoff does the same among all three factors, depending upon the occupation and time point. Specific details are available from the author upon request, of course. Most important, these disparities do not particularly threaten the analysis which follows, because (a) this discussion is unavoidably limited to a level of "rights," "arbitration," and "(in)security" anyway (i.e., as opposed to assertions based upon a singular policy provision), (b) strike policy is likely to be made, regardless of its placement in either of the two "bundles," and (c) dues checkoff, as contended in the text, is observed to be relatively uniform across states irrespective of their adoption of or hostility to a structured bargaining framework in general.

9. This is a cross-occupational mean observed in the data. Disaggregated, strikes are prohibited for state employees by 64 percent of all jurisdictions, for police by 74 percent, for firefighters by 78 percent, for teachers by 66 percent, and by 58 percent for other local employees.

10. Because factor scores were substituted for raw data, a discussion of relative contributions made by the exogenous variables would appear to be more informative than one based upon unstandardized parameter estimates. Hence the reporting procedure in table 5.5.

11. The first of these two types of strikes seems to be less frequent today than it was in an earlier era. A quick cross-tabulation of the data indicates that only 5 percent of all (5000 +) strikes observed during the period studied here occurred in the Right-to-Work states, the jurisdictions which would seem most likely to suffer them. This suggests that cutting organizing activity off at the knees may be the best way for policymakers to avoid service disruption.

12. In fact, a stepwise regression of strikes upon diffusion, unionization, and policy indicated that diffusion alone explains 58 percent of the variance in the dependent variable. The others improve the variance explained by no greater than three percent as they enter the equations. As before, these results are not included in order to avoid redundancy.

13. All differences are real, to the extent that complete data for the fifty states during the years studied are employed. See Barrilleaux and Miller, 1988, especially note 9, p. 1103, for a discussion quite relevant to this line of inquiry in general.

Appendix 5.1   Additional Methodological Notes

Four issues associated with the character of the Valletta and Freeman policy data (described in table 3.1) require explanation, given their importance to the analyses pursued in chapters 4 and 5.

ISSUE 1

The Problem

A continuing weakness of the past research is the fact that it so often ignores policy differentials across subsets of the public workforce. That subnational jurisdictions treat "essential" service personnel somewhat differently than they do others has been documented. The fix, however, complicates matters. It means that disaggregated data like these, while more precise, make it difficult to measure association between the character of the grand policy environment and state-level outcomes (e.g., the relationship between general policy intent and the degree of bargaining which actually results).

The Fix

In order to examine such aggregate-level relationships, an additive index was constructed across the policy measures in table 3.1, using the reformulated (i.e., negative to positive) scores and the operations described in chapter 4. Following Kochan's lead (1973, p. 325), three tests were conducted to assess the internal consistency of the outcomes. In the first, correlations between each of the fourteen indicators and the additive measure were run, across occupations and time points. The mean result was a .59 level of correlation, with a .31 standard deviation. Weak correlations associated with the union shop and strike policy variables were responsible for this less-than-reassuring outcome. One assessment is that these two indicators exhibit among the least variation of the fourteen over time, thereby constraining the magnitude of the coefficient. When they are removed from the calculation, Pearson's r increases to .70, with a .17 standard deviation (a figure slightly less than that reported by Kochan). In the second test, policy scores for each occupation and year were correlated with the appropriate cross-occupational measure. The mean correlation here was .95, with a .03 standard deviation. Cronbach's alpha was calculated as a third check. Though the result was a coefficient of .90, the applicability of this test is limited, given the variation in indicators and the multidimensional nature of the policy measure exhibited in table 5.4 (see Carmines and Zeller, 1979, for a discussion). Results on reliability are therefore mixed. This makeshift construction does receive support in the draft codebook accompanying the data.

ISSUE 2

The Problem

In discussing this research with a variety of colleagues, the Valletta and Freeman scale quite often draws remarks about the continuum of numbers assigned the provisions in table 3.1. Many feel (or insist) that the prohibitions therein should be reassigned a negative value.

The Fix

The reformulation utilized throughout (and described in chapter 4) was born of this skepticism, after most of the estimation reported in chapters 4 and 5 had already been accomplished using the original values. Direct comparison in results was facilitated as the many tables and figures therein were redrawn. The verdict is that the reformulation led to only marginal differences in the patterns observed. In fact, correlations between the reformulated scores and the original ones are perfect or near perfect. The only exceptions are union shop, agency shop, and strike policy; their relatively invariant nature across the large N is once again the suspected cause.

ISSUE 3

The Problem

The gap between policy and practice widens to the extent that local jurisdictions of sufficient autonomy adopt bargaining mechanisms that differ from state policy. As has been suggested two or three times in the text, Missouri provides only meet-and-confer rights to its public employees, but the City of Columbia negotiates with its workforce anyway. The tradeoff between internal and external validity is therefore quite tangible here.

The Fix

The critical assumption required is that state policy is the single most important indicator of the bargaining environment facing public employees within its confines. There is little question that most cities do defer to the state, making this leap of faith less treacherous than it might at first appear.

ISSUE 4

The Problem

Finally, there is a potential level of measurement issue relevant as well. Table 3.1 should make it apparent that the data are arguably ordinal, to the extent that a one-unit increase on any specific indicator is in the direction of an environment characterized by greater structure and permissiveness, particularly after the reformulation of the scoring method. The level of measurement traditionally determines statistic selection.

The Fix

The ordinal-interval debate rages on among social scientists. The analyses reported in the text employ mechanics intended for use with interval level data primarily because there is little difference in the order of magnitude between lambda, gamma, and Pearson's r in most cases anyway. Using factor analysis with these data may be a bigger problem. Its implications continue to be investigated.

There is no question that these are important issues, which is why they are explicit. Though social scientists prefer scalpels, they are often limited to cleavers.

6 Summary and Conclusions

Collective bargaining is a relatively new development in the public sector. It emerged first in the middle 1950s and then took off by the late 1960s and early 1970s. During and since that time, subnational policymakers have been engaged in some interesting and important experimentation with a wide range of policy measures designed to regulate the labor-management relationship in their jurisdictions. With the states and localities as their laboratories, legislators, executive branch officials, and judges have wrestled long and hard with questions of whether and how to establish a workable and mutually advantageous system of shared responsibility for the operation of the public workplace with their employees.

Collective bargaining in government seems to have reached the end of an adolescence. Having concluded a phase of rapid growth by about 1980, it is now time to look forward, toward what these systems that decision makers have constructed will become in the future. Stasis is unlikely. If it was labor's vitality which played a significant role in the quantum growth of policy and a much-debated decline in its health which helped to slow the rate of change, then the legal environment can be expected to remain in flux as unionism finds its place in an evolving political economy.

Research efforts to explain the phenomenon can be described in much the same fashion. The significance of the public side of bargaining was recognized early, which led to a large number of analyses. In the flurry of activity which followed, it was economics that dominated scholars' attentions. Wage studies by labor economists make up the biggest portion of the research completed thus far. Those analysts concerned with alternative dimensions of the process produced a great deal of mixed evidence across a limited range of observations. Lest this criticism be too harsh, it must be added that these pioneers were forced to rely heavily upon the kindness of strangers. Accessible data describing union activity and bargaining outcomes waxed and waned with the level of interest in the Bureau of Labor Statistics and in the White House—a constraint which continues. A clearer picture of policy itself did not develop until recently, and only then because of the support of an external benefactor as well (i.e., a grant from the Sloan Foundation to the National Bureau of Economic Research).

It is especially surprising that political scientists have so infrequently embraced the many theoretical and practical questions associated with the public side of collective bargaining, a topic with significant implications for the quality of governance and one, therefore, of natural appeal for those members of the discipline most interested in policy and administration. Two dimensions stand out in particular. First, collective bargaining is about power; namely, (1) the degree to which jurisdictions are willing and able to provide their employees with voice in work issues, and (2) the possibility that the latter will achieve enough political strength to win much more often than they lose, regardless of legal intentions and actions to the contrary. Second, it is the aim and the virtue of the policy analyst to reduce uncertainty for those charged with responsibility for public institutions—to the extent, of course, that communication between the two occurs.

This research project was conceived of these origins. It represents an attempt to get a better handle on the basic shape, causes, and consequences of subnational policy at this apparent cusp of labor history. It further explores, replicates, and augments the work of the past in an effort to provide a firmer grasp of what we know and what we do not know about public sector collective bargaining across years, states, and functions. The central contention is that better baseline understanding will not only improve upon a quite fragmented view of the phenomenon, but that it can also be the springboard for more elaborate testing now and in the context of future developments.

This book is probably best described as an interim report on the progress made to date toward accomplishing a much larger research agenda. Both are organized around three simple yet compelling charges for policy analysis: to determine what governments do, why they do it, and what difference it makes. The results thus far are summarized below.

MAJOR FINDINGS

What Governments Do

The descriptive statistics presented in chapter 3 allow three categories of generalization.

1.   In general:

(a)   Collective bargaining began its spread across the states during the 1950s. The biggest push toward adoption began about 1970; the rate of change decreased by 1980.

(b)   There are some categories of potential policy action which are not utilized by decision makers across the time points examined here. No state prohibits dues checkoff, mediation, or fact-finding; only one outlaws arbitration (for a brief span of time); none makes union shop compulsory.

(c)   Policy remains somewhat underdeveloped. Something less than a majority have constructed comprehensive frameworks for collective bargaining with their employees.

2.   In the context of specific policy provisions, it is observed that:

(a)   There was a decided move toward bargaining across the states between 1955 and 1984. An implied duty to bargain on the part of management was the most frequent outcome by 1975; when combined with those states making this obligation explicit, mandated negotiation became the majority outcome across governments.

(b)   In terms of bargaining scope, a majority made compensation a negotiable subject by 1975.

(c)   Among those speaking to the details of representation and election, all but one state at any time point provided exclusive recognition to the majority labor organization. The bias clearly continues to favor explicit certification mechanisms.

(d)   The term of recognition appears to have been frequently neglected in policy deliberations, yet a twelve-month election bar is the preferred choice among adopters (from or regardless of contract expiration).

(e)   A majority emerges to address agency shop only by 1980. The most frequent outcome is an explicit prohibition, but approximately one-quarter of all jurisdictions make it negotiable and a small number choose the compulsory route.

(f)   Dues checkoff seems to be a popular concession. Though a majority of the states have not addressed it, there is a fairly even split between those making automatic deduction negotiable and their counterparts, who define it as a compulsory management obligation.

(g)   Their formal position on union shop indicates that subnational policymakers are quite antagonistic to compulsory union membership. At maximum only a small handful make such provisions negotiable at any time point.

(h)   The incidence of Right-to-Work laws increased 50 percent during the period of study. Most of this change occurred by 1965.

(i)   Of the impasse resolution procedures, states find mediation most appealing. They choose also to make it easily accessible: most frequently the PERB or PERC may initiate it either unilaterally or upon the request of either party to a dispute.

(j)   Policymakers demonstrate less interest in fact-finding. Like mediation, it is most often provided on a discretionary basis among those choosing this third-party option.

(k)   Arbitration receives the least attention, and there is less consensus about the proper means of its initiation as well. The majority view among those taking a position is that all negotiable issues should be included in this step, yet the states show little desire to experiment with its unconventional forms.

(l)   It is something of a surprise that about one-quarter of all subnational governments take no stance on strikes at any time point. It is no shock, however, that approximately two-thirds of those acting on the issue ban them (with or without explicit sanctions).

3.   These data also allow a view of similarities and differences across occupations. The modal state (acting in about 1970) is most likely to establish an implied duty to bargain across a range of issues which includes compensation; it also outlaws union shop and strikes (the latter without explicit penalties). There are exceptions, however:

(a)   Nearly twice as many jurisdictions prohibit bargaining for state workers as for all other personnel. They represent a similar exception where scope is concerned, as they are not included in the majority making compensation negotiable in 1975. Along with teachers, most states allow automatic dues deduction for this group. And like their teaching and "other local" counterparts, they face arbitration based upon two-party consent most often.

(b)   Uniformed personnel are treated differently than other employees. A large majority of states allow firefighters to negotiate compensation. Arbitration is used most often in both police and fire services, usually on a discretionary or mandatory basis and across all negotiable issues. Both groups are most likely to face a strike ban as well.

(c)   As with firefighters, a majority of subnational governments specify the term of recognition facing teachers' organizations explicitly in the law. As it is with state employees, teachers get dues checkoff in a majority of states as well. They were the only occupation for which more than half of all jurisdictions allowed fact-finding in some guise between 1980 and 1984. This group is also most likely to face specific penalties when they strike.

Why They Do It

In chapter 4 various hypotheses derived from a small literature on antecedents are retested. Expanding the number of time points considered and employing a more complete picture of policy leads to:

1. Support for the "conventional wisdom" that more liberal (conservative) states are more (less) likely to institutionalize a collective bargaining relationship with their public employees.
2. Evidence to suggest that the additional suspects identified heretofore in the cumulative research—urbanization, income and expenditures per capita, innovation, and unionization—play a significant and reasonably consistent role in policy determination within and between the occupations studied.

What Difference It Makes

Chapter 5 speaks to the more compelling issue of policy consequences. Hypotheses involving the two variables of greatest relevance to policy makers—union growth and service disruption—receive further testing as well. This portion of the analysis indicates that:

1. Policymakers make three sets of decisions. They seem to develop a system of basic collective bargaining rights, they consider union security issues, and arbitration receives special attention as well.
2. A reasonably strong link exists between policy and union membership, particularly in terms of the variance explained in the latter by the rights and arbitration factors.
3. A more complex relationship exists between policy and service disruption. Policy appears to have an important relationship to the diffusion of bargaining, to which in turn the frequency of disruption may be tied.
4. A direct link exists between policy and disruption as well. The latter covaries with the degree of the public employer's obligation, the treatment of strikes, and the availability of arbitration;
5. Changing or different relationships exist between occupations and over time.

CONCLUSIONS

Taken together, these results suggest at least three conclusions: (1) that public policymakers recognize both the benefits and the costs associated with collective bargaining, (2) that the major variables identified by the literature play important roles in determining the legal environment, and (3) that unionization and service disruption vary with policy as well when the latter is treated as an independent variable.

The first idea is quite visible by the end of chapter 3. Policymakers attempt to establish a labor-management relationship in a variety of ways for their jurisdictions. The cross-state result is an expansion of collective bargaining since 1955, an expansion which incorporates specific actions designed to empower employees while attempting to regulate the potential for dysfunctions to occur.

Some subnational governments do not participate in this trend. Because the exceptions are most always more interesting than the rule, chapter 4 examines the variance in policy adoption among the states. The findings here lead to the second conclusion. Renewed support for an ideological explanation of the phenomenon is the initial finding. A series of determination models explain a substantial proportion of the variance when appropriate controls and time are considered. In the context of manipulable variables, the evidence reaffirms a policy proverb well known to Saul Alinsky, Mancur Olson, and the union entrepreneur: as ye organize, so shall ye reap.

The third conclusion is equally straightforward. The outcome of chapter 5 is the sense that (1) policymakers might make it easier or more difficult for unionization to occur, and (2) strike propensities change across categories of policy as well. These findings offer hope to subnational public decision makers that their actions may indeed make a difference.

Both the casual and the careful reader of this research could be alarmed by what it says. From the former might come the classic complaint that academics of all shapes and sizes spend most of their time reinventing the wheel. The simplest response to such a criticism is that it does not apply here. Because only sketchy snapshots were available until very recently, the comparative view of the state labor relations environment lacked a good deal of precision, its specific shapes unclear. The presentation and interpretation of the Valletta and Freeman data performed in chapter 3 are therefore worthwhile. Though it is not difficult to posit a long list of hypotheses relevant to the issue of policy determination, none received much more than very limited testing in an extremely small literature prior to this reexamination. Third, a similar problem was identified in the context of policy impacts. While it is reassuring to believe that policy matters, or the opposite, the review of the cumulative scholarship on collective bargaining presented in chapter 5 provides just cause to accept either assertion.

On the other hand, there are plenty of good reasons to approach these conclusions with skepticism. The careful reader will recognize, accurately, the importance of the many assumptions upon which this analysis is built. More compelling is the need for further testing of the links established here in light of causal uncertainties, competing hypotheses, and alternative specifications of the models which are employed. Such is the nature of social science in general and quasi experimentation in particular.

These issues about contribution are raised not to serve as a defensive sort of apology. Rather, they are intended to point toward a direction for future research. Its boundaries are identified in the final section of this chapter.

A RESEARCH AGENDA

A wide array of interesting and significant ideas, issues, and questions associated with collective bargaining in the public sector merit further study. Three stand out as quite pressing. Most immediate is thorough comprehension of policy impacts. If an important stride toward nailing down the bivariate links between the legal environment, unionization, and disruption has been achieved, it covers only a limited time period. The analysis requires expansion at both ends in order to capture the pre–1972 and post–1980 phenomenon. The lack of a longitudinal string of comparable data for these years is the first obstacle which must be overcome. Augmenting the number of observations available for a broader view of this sort would be a costly, yet rewarding, enterprise.

This point is particularly true if the many questions associated with causation left unanswered by this research are to approach resolution. For example, whether unionization drives policy or the reverse remains quite uncertain. Nor is a verdict on cause and effect with respect to service disruption delivered here—only covariation is assessed. These data are necessary to extending our grasp.

The second step involves three components: the world is not a bivariate place, nor is it uniformly linear and nonrecursive. The dependent variables of central interest (e.g., strikes in particular) demand better modeling across a wider range of theoretical determinants and with tests of greater validity and rigor. Though mostly implicit at the time, the ability to generalize about the findings in the literature presented in chapter 5 was hindered as much by wide variation in technique as it was by differences in operationalization and unit of analysis. Greater consistency of approach across a wider range of observations is required if true findings are to be distinguished from artifacts induced by specification error. This statement should not be misread: it is less a sort of naive attempt to ordain methodology than it is an expression of concern about an observed atomization which very much hinders cumulative understanding of the phenomenon—a significant interest of this research.

Third, there is no question that the range of foci captured by the lens requires expansion as well. Collective bargaining has implications for many facets of governance not considered here and not explained adequately in the literature. As detailed in chapter 2, the direction of its impact upon productivity remains indeterminate. Equally worrisome is the fact that while public unions are often attributed with a great deal of significance, actual understanding of their relationship to the many tasks assigned to public personnel management is weak or nonexistent. These two sets of outcome questions by no means exhaust the range of organizational issues for which collective bargaining has relevance. Transcending administration, labor's changing role in the larger political process necessitates continuous monitoring as well.

It is this last concern—the place of organized labor in American democracy—which is, of course, the ultimate source of relevance for this research enterprise. These analyses provide some important clues to policymakers about the means through which they might regulate labor-management relations in their jurisdictions. The broad significance lies in the vitality of the pluralist process, an issue of greater depth and complexity than that contained in the narrower focus defined here.

The implication of these results is that the health of the system will depend upon the skill with which policymakers use the tools available to them. Equally important are the value preferences which comprise the ends to which they target their actions. The link between policy and unionization seems strong enough in chapters 4 and 5, for example, that labor organizations can make or break, or can be made or broken by, the course established in the legal environment. The uncertainty exhibited in this last statement reflects, of course, causal uncertainties. Strict and enforced strike bans may have similar or more severe repercussions. The quality of management-employee interaction, the costs and benefits therein, and the degree to which labor is represented in the political process hang in the balance.

Policymakers will, and should, adjust the levers of control they possess in ways which will allow them to pursue the values to which they subscribe. Maintaining the fairness of the playing field is only one such value. In large measure, the political system is only as healthy as it remains in state and local government. Labor's power, relative to that possessed by other competitors for scarce public goods and across varying policy contexts, constitutes the research focus of central import in the long run.

Unions in the United States are not dead, but their place in society has and will continue to be transformed by domestic and international developments. The labor movement has been an important part of American history and culture, but its role in her future is quite difficult to predict at this juncture. It is hard to envision a scenario in which collective economic activity by the working class is absent. It seems equally unlikely that unions and their leadership, public and private, can survive the crisis of credibility they face at present without major structural or environmental change. The future of collective bargaining is uncertain, which makes analysis of its relationship to policy necessary, complicated, and exciting.

Bibliography

Aboud, Antone, and Grace S. Aboud. 1974. *The Right to Strike in Public Employment.* New York: Cornell University Press.

Ashenfelter, Orley C., and Ronald G. Ehrenberg. 1975. "The Demand for Labor in the Public Sector." In *Labor in the Public and Nonprofit Sectors*, ed. Daniel S. Hamermesh. Princeton, N.J.: Princeton University Press.

Baird, Charles W. 1986. "Strikes Against Government: The California Supreme Court Decision." *Government Union Review* 1:1–29.

Balfour, Alan, and Alexander Holmes. 1981. "The Effectiveness of No Strike Laws for Public School Teachers." *Journal of Collective Negotiations in the Public Sector* 10:133–144.

Barrilleaux, Charles J., and Mark E. Miller. 1988. "The Political Economy of State Medicaid Policy." *American Political Science Review* 82:1089–1107.

Bent, Alan E., and T. Zane Reeves. 1978. *Collective Bargaining in the Public Sector.* Menlo Park, Calif.: Benjamin/Cummings.

Bentley, Arthur F. 1908. *The Process of Government.* Chicago: University of Chicago Press.

Bluestone, Barry, and Bennett Harrison. 1982. *The Deindustrialization of America.* New York: Basic Books.

Braybrooke, David, and Charles E. Lindblom. 1963. *A Strategy of Decision.* New York: Free Press.

Burton, John F., and Terry Thomason. 1988. "The Extent of Collective Bargaining in the Public Sector." In *Public Sector Bargaining*, ed. Benjamin Aaron et al. Washington, D.C.: Bureau of National Affairs.

———, and Charles E. Krider. 1975. "The Incidence of Strikes in Public Employment." In *Labor in the Public and Nonprofit Sectors*, ed. Daniel S. Hamermesh. Princeton, N.J.: Princeton University Press.

———, and Charles E. Krider. 1972. "The Roles and Consequences of Strikes by Public Employees." In *Collective Bargaining in Government*, ed. Joseph J.

Lowenberg and Michael H. Moskow. Englewood Cliffs, N.J.: Prentice-Hall.

Carmines, Edward G., and Richard A. Zeller. 1979. *Reliability and Validity Assessment.* Beverly Hills, Calif.: Sage.

Cayer, N. Joseph. 1986. *Public Personnel Administration in the United States.* New York: St. Martin's.

Cobb, Roger W., and Charles D. Elder. 1983. *Participation in American Politics.* Baltimore: Johns Hopkins University Press.

Colton, David L. 1978. "Collective Bargaining Laws and Teacher Strikes." *Journal of Collective Negotiations in the Public Sector* 7:201–212.

Conant, John L. 1989. "Agency Problems in Public Sector Labor Relations." *Government Union Review* 10:40–54.

Congressional Quarterly. 1985. "Interest Groups Give Members Their Grades." *Congressional Quarterly Weekly Report* 43:747–749.

———. 1984. "Lobbies Issue Congressional Report Cards." *Congressional Quarterly Weekly Report* 42:1695–1697.

———. 1983. "Interest Groups Rate Members of Congress." *Congressional Quarterly Weekly Report* 41:905–907.

———. 1982. "Interest Groups Rate Members of Congress." *Congressional Quarterly Weekly Report* 40:1614–1617.

———. 1981. "Congressional Rating Game is Hard to Win." *Congressional Quarterly Weekly Report* 39:516–518.

———. 1980. " 'Liberal' Senators Facing Tough Reelection Fights Moderated Their 1979 Votes." *Congressional Quarterly Weekly Report* 38:1117–1119.

———. 1979. "Tough Election Fights Forced Some Members to Moderate Their Stands." *Congressional Quarterly Weekly Report* 37:1067–1069.

———. 1978. "House Members' Votes Show Conservative Trend." *Congressional Quarterly Weekly Report* 36:914–916.

———. 1977. "Group Ratings: A Year of Dissatisfaction." *Congressional Quarterly Weekly Report* 35:220–222.

———. 1976. "Group Ratings: Liberals' Impact Diluted." *Congressional Quarterly Weekly Report* 34:1291–1293.

———. 1975. "Group Ratings: Trend To Liberalization Seen." *Congressional Quarterly Weekly Report* 33:389–391.

———. 1974. "Pressure Group Ratings of All Members of Congress." *Congressional Quarterly Weekly Report* 32:815–817.

———. 1972. "Pressure Group Ratings of All Members of Congress." *Congressional Quarterly Weekly Report* 30:931–933, 3111–3113.

———. 1971. "Pressure Groups Rate Each Senator, Representative." *Congressional Quarterly Weekly Report* 29:865–867.

———. 1970. "Pressure Groups Rate Each Senator, Representative." *Congressional Quarterly Weekly Report* 28:569–571.

———. 1968. "Nonparty Groups Rate Each Senator, Representative." *Congressional Quarterly Weekly Report* 26:917–919, 3197–3199.

———. 1966. "Two Liberal, Three Conservative Groups Rate Congress." *Congressional Quarterly Weekly Report* 24:472–474, 2764–2766.

———. 1964. "Nonparty Groups Rate Each Senator, Representative." *Congressional Quarterly Weekly Report* 22:2546–2548.

————. 1962. "Nonparty Groups Rate Each Senator, Representative." *Congressional Quarterly Weekly Report* 20:2022–2024.

————. 1960. "Nonparty Groups Seek to Influence Congressional Races." *Congressional Quarterly Weekly Report* 18:1659–1661.

Cook, James. 1983. "The Argument for Plant Closing Legislation." *Forbes* 31:82–84.

Dahl, Robert A. 1961. *Who Governs?*. New Haven, Conn.: Yale University Press.

Dalton, Amy H. 1984. "The Organization of State and Local Government Employees: Reply." *Journal of Labor Research* 5:201–204.

————. 1982. "A Theory of the Organization of State and Local Government Employees." *Journal of Labor Research* 3:163–176.

Dawson, Richard E., and James A. Robinson. 1963. "Interparty Competition, Economic Variables, and Welfare Policies in the American States." *Journal of Politics* 25:265–289.

Denhardt, Robert B. 1984. *Theories of Public Organization*. Monterey, Calif.: Brooks/Cole.

Ducat, Craig R., and Harold W. Chase. 1988. *Constitutional Interpretation*. St. Paul, Minn.: West.

Dye, Thomas R. 1979. "Politics Versus Economics: The Development of the Literature on Policy Determination." *Policy Studies Journal* 7:652–662.

————. 1966. *Politics, Economics, and the Public*. Chicago: Rand McNally.

Easton, David. 1953. *The Political System*. New York: Alfred A. Knopf.

Edwards, Harry T. 1973. "The Emerging Duty to Bargain in the Public Sector." *Michigan Law Review* 71:885, 895–896.

Faber, Charles F., and Donald L. Martin. 1979. "Two Factors Affecting Enactment of Collective Bargaining Legislation in Public Education." *Journal of Collective Negotiations in the Public Sector* 8:151–159.

Fallon, Robert. 1977. "The Effects of Public Policy on the Incidence of Public Sector Strikes." Unpublished manuscript. Harvard University Economics, no. 1650.

Federal Labor Relations Authority. 1981. *A Guide to the Federal Service Labor Management Relations Statute*. Washington, DC: U.S. Government Printing Office.

Felker, Lon. 1986. "Public Sector Labor Relations in the States and Municipalities: The Impact of Union Legislative Environment." *Public Personnel Management* 15:41–50.

Fossum, John A. 1989. *Labor Relations*. Homewood, Ill.: Richard D. Irwin.

Freedman, Audrey. 1979. *Managing Labor Relations*. New York: The Conference Board.

Freeman, Richard B. 1986. "Unionism Comes to the Public Sector." *Journal of Economic Literature* 24:41–86.

Ginsberg, Benjamin, and Martin Shefter. 1985. "The New Politics, the Reconstituted Right, and the 1984 Election." In *The Elections of 1984*, ed. Michael Nelson. Washington, D.C.: Congressional Quarterly.

Goldfield, Michael. 1990. "Public Sector Union Growth and Public Policy." *Policy Studies Journal* 18:404–420.

————, and Jonathan Plotkin. 1987. "Public Sector Unionism in the United States: The Reasons for its Take-Off in the Early 1960s." Unpublished manuscript. Midwest Political Science Association.

Gordon, George J. 1986. *Public Administration in America*. New York: St. Martin's.

Grodin, Joseph R., Donald H. Wollett, and Reginald H. Alleyne, Jr. 1979. *Collective Bargaining in Public Employment*. Washington, D.C.: Bureau of National Affairs.

Hofferbert, Richard I. 1968. ''Socioeconomic Dimensions of the American States: 1890–1960.'' *Midwest Journal of Political Science* 12:401–418.

———. 1966. ''The Relationship Between Public Policy and Some Structural and Environmental Variables in the American States.'' *American Political Science Review* 60:73–82.

Holley, William H., and Kenneth M. Jennings. 1980. *The Labor Relations Process.* Hinsdale, Ill.: Dryden.

Hopkins, Anne H., George E. Rawson, and Russell L. Smith. 1976. ''Public Employee Unionization in the States.'' *Administration and Society* 8:319–341.

Horn, Robert N., William J. McGuire, and Joseph Tomkiewicz. 1982a. ''An Empirical Model of Strike Activity by Teachers.'' *Journal of Collective Negotiations in the Public Sector* 11:155–164.

———. 1982b. ''Work Stoppages by Teachers: An Empirical Analysis.'' *Journal of Labor Research* 3:487–496.

Ichniowski, Casey. 1982. ''Arbitration and Police Bargaining: Prescriptions for the Blue Flu.'' *Industrial Relations* 21:149–166.

International Personnel Management Association. 1989. ''Police and Firefighter Bargaining Bills Introduced.'' *IPMA News* (July):8.

Klauser, Jack E. 1977. ''Public Sector Impasse Resolution in Hawaii.'' *Industrial Relations* 16:283–289.

Kochan, Thomas A. 1980. *Collective Bargaining and Industrial Relations.* Homewood, Ill.: Richard D. Irwin.

———. 1973. ''Correlates of State Public Employee Bargaining Laws.'' *Industrial Relations* 12:322–337.

Marshall, Alfred. 1936. *Principles of Economics.* New York: Macmillan.

Martin, Daniel W. 1988. ''The Fading Legacy of Woodrow Wilson.'' *Public Administration Review* 48:631–636.

Mass, Michael A., and Anita F. Gottlieb. 1979. ''Federally Legislated Collective Bargaining for State and Local Governments: A Logical Imperative.'' In *Labor Relations in the Public Sector*, ed. Marvin J. Levine and Eugene C. Hagburg. Salt Lake City, Utah: Brighton.

Methe, David T., and James L. Perry. 1980. ''The Impacts of Collective Bargaining on Local Government Services: A Review of Research.'' *Public Administration Review* 40:359–371.

Moore, William J. 1978. ''An Analysis of Teacher Union Growth.'' *Industrial Relations* 17:204–215.

———. 1977. ''Factors Affecting Growth in Public and Private Sector Unions.'' *Journal of Collective Negotiations in the Public Sector* 6:37–43.

———, and R.J. Newman. 1975. ''On the Prospects for American Trade Union Growth.'' *Review of Economics and Statistics* 57:435–445.

Nigro, Felix A., and Lloyd G. Nigro. 1986. *The New Public Personnel Administration.* Itasca, Ill.: F.E. Peacock.

Osigweh, Chimezie A.B. 1985. ''Collective Bargaining and Public Sector Union Power.'' *Public Personnel Management* 14:75–84.

Reagan, Michael D., and John G. Sanzone. 1981. *The New Federalism.* New York: Oxford University Press.

Redenius, Charles. 1976. ''Public Employees: A Survey of Some Critical Problems on the Frontier of Collective Bargaining.'' *Labor Law Journal* 27:588–599.

Reid, Joseph D., Jr., and Michael Kurth. 1984: "The Organization of State and Local Government Employees: A Comment on Dalton." *Journal of Labor Research* 5:191–199.

Reynolds, Lloyd G., Stanley H. Masters, and Colletta H. Moser. 1991. *Labor Economics and Labor Relations*. Englewood Cliffs, N.J.: Prentice Hall.

Rodgers, Robert C. 1980. "A Replication of the Burton-Krider Model of Public Employee Strike Activity." In *Proceedings of the Thirty-Third Annual Meeting*, ed. Barbara A. Dennis. Denver, Colo.: Industrial Relations Research Association.

Rosenbloom, David H. 1989. *Public Administration*. New York: Random House.

Sabatier, Paul A., and Daniel Mazmanian. 1980. "Policy Implementation: A Framework of Analysis." *Policy Studies Journal* 8:538–560.

Salisbury, Robert H. 1969. "An Exchange Theory of Interest Groups." *Midwest Journal of Political Science* 13:1–32.

Saltzman, Gregory M. 1985. "Bargaining Laws as a Cause and Consequence of the Growth of Teacher Unionism." *Industrial and Labor Relations Review* 38:335–351.

Schlosstein, Ralph. 1975. "State and Local Government Finances During Recession." *Challenge* 18:1–10.

Schneider, Saundra K. 1982. "Patterns of Social Policy Development in Four Welfare States." Unpublished manuscript. Midwest Political Science Association.

Schuman, David, and Dick W. Olufs III. 1988. *Public Administration in the United States*. Lexington, Mass.: D.C. Heath.

Seroka, Jim. 1985. "The Determinants of Public Employee Union Growth." *Review of Public Personnel Administration* 5:5–20.

Shafritz, Jay M., Albert C. Hyde, and David H. Rosenbloom. 1986. *Personnel Management in Government*. New York: Marcel Dekker.

Sharkansky, Ira, and Richard I. Hofferbert. 1969. "Dimensions of State Politics, Economics, and Public Policy." *American Political Science Review* 63:867–880.

Stanfield, Rochelle. 1981. "For the States, It's Time to Put Up or Shut Up on Federal Block Grants." *National Journal* 13:1800.

Starling, Grover. 1982. *Managing the Public Sector*. Homewood, Ill.: Dorsey.

Stern, James L., and Craig Olson. 1982. "The Propensity to Strike of Local Government Employees." *Journal of Collective Negotiations in the Public Sector* 11:201–214.

Sylvia, Ronald D. 1989. *Critical Issues in Public Personnel Policy*. Pacific Grove, Calif.: Brooks/Cole.

Thurow, Lester C. 1980. *The Zero-Sum Society*. New York: Penguin.

Tiebout, Charles M. 1956. "A Pure Theory of Local Expenditures." *Journal of Political Economy* 64:416–424.

Troy, Leo, and Neil Sheflin. 1985. *Union Sourcebook*. West Orange, N.J.: Industrial Relations Information Services.

Truman, David. 1951. *The Governmental Process*. New York: Alfred A. Knopf.

U.S. Department of Commerce, Bureau of the Census. 1987. *Statistical Abstract of the United States*. Washington, D.C.: U.S. Government Printing Office.

———. 1986. *Statistical Abstract of the United States*. Washington, D.C.: U.S. Government Printing Office.

———. 1985. *Statistical Abstract of the United States*. Washington, D.C.: U.S. Government Printing Office.

———. 1984. *Statistical Abstract of the United States*. Washington, D.C.: U.S. Government Printing Office.

————. 1982. *Census of Governments.* Washington, D.C.: U.S. Government Printing Office.

————. 1981. *Statistical Abstract of the United States.* Washington, D.C.: U.S. Government Printing Office.

————. 1980. *Labor Management Relations in State and Local Government.* Washington, D.C.: U.S. Government Printing Office.

————. 1980. *Statistical Abstract of the United States.* Washington, D.C.: U.S. Government Printing Office.

————. 1979. *Labor Management Relations in State and Local Government.* Washington, D.C.: U.S. Government Printing Office.

————. 1979. *Statistical Abstract of the United States.* Washington, D.C.: U.S. Government Printing Office.

————. 1978. *Labor Management Relations in State and Local Government.* Washington, D.C.: U.S. Government Printing Office.

————. 1978. *Statistical Abstract of the United States.* Washington, D.C.: U.S. Government Printing Office.

————. 1977. *Census of Governments.* Washington, D.C.: U.S. Government Printing Office.

————. 1977. *Statistical Abstract of the United States.* Washington, D.C.: U.S. Government Printing Office.

————. 1976. *Labor Management Relations in State and Local Government.* Washington, D.C.: U.S. Government Printing Office.

————. 1976. *Statistical Abstract of the United States.* Washington, D.C.: U.S. Government Printing Office.

————. 1975. *Labor Management Relations in State and Local Government.* Washington, D.C.: U.S. Government Printing Office.

————. 1975. *Statistical Abstract of the United States.* Washington, D.C.: U.S. Government Printing Office.

————. 1974. *Labor Management Relations in State and Local Government.* Washington, D.C.: U.S. Government Printing Office.

————. 1974. *Statistical Abstract of the United States.* Washington, D.C.: U.S. Government Printing Office.

————. 1973. *Statistical Abstract of the United States.* Washington, D.C.: U.S. Government Printing Office.

————. 1972. *Census of Governments.* Washington, D.C.: U.S. Government Printing Office.

————. 1972. *Labor Management Relations in State and Local Government.* Washington, D.C.: U.S. Government Printing Office.

U.S. Department of Labor, Bureau of Labor Statistics. 1981. "Summary of State Labor Laws." *Government Employee Relations Reporter* 51:501–530.

Valletta, Robert G., and Richard B. Freeman. 1985. *National Bureau of Economic Research Collective Bargaining Law Data Set.* Cambridge, Mass.: National Bureau of Economic Research.

Veglahn, Peter A. 1983. "Public Sector Strike Penalties and Their Appeal." *Public Personnel Management* 12:196–205.

Walker, Jack L. "Innovation in State Politics." 1971. In *Politics in the American States,* ed. Herbert Jacob and Kenneth N. Vines. Boston: Little Brown.

Weinstock, Henry R., and Paul Van Horn. 1969. "Impact of Negotiations Upon Public Education." *The Clearing House* (February):358–363.

Weintraub, Andrew R., and Robert J. Thornton. 1976. "Why Teachers Strike: The Economic and Legal Determinants." *Journal of Collective Negotiations in the Public Sector* 5:193–206.

Weitzman, Joan P. 1979. "The Effects of Economic Restraints on Public Sector Collective Bargaining: The Lessons from New York City." In *Government Labor Relations: Trends and Information for the Future*, ed. Hugh D. Jascourt. Oak Park, Ill.: Moore.

Wellington, Harry H., and Ralph K. Winter. 1971. *The Unions and the Cities*. Washington, D.C.: Brookings Institution.

———. 1970. "Structuring Collective Bargaining in Public Employment." *Yale Law Journal* 79:805–870.

———. 1969. "The Limits of Collective Bargaining in Public Employment." *Yale Law Journal* 78:1107–1127.

Wheeler, Hoyt N. 1975. "An Analysis of Fire Fighter Strikes." *Labor Law Journal* 26:17–20.

Index

ABOUT THE AUTHOR

John Patrick Piskulich is currently an assistant professor of political science at Oakland University. He was educated at the University of Missouri-Columbia and the State University of New York at Binghamton. The American Association of University Professors is the fifth (and only public) union of which he has been a member.